COMMUNICATING
AT THE TOP

COMMUNICATING AT THE TOP

What you need to know about communicating to run an organization

GEORGE DE MARE

JOHN WILEY & SONS
New York · Chichester · Brisbane · Toronto

Library of Congress Cataloging in Publication Data:

De Mare, George.
    Communicating at the top.

    Rev. version of the work published in 1967 under
title: Communicating for leadership.
    Includes index.
    1.   Communication in management.   I.   Title.
HF5718.D45   1979   658.4'5   78-31951
ISBN 0-471-05681-2

Printed in the United States of America

10 9 8 7 6 5 4 3 2 1

to
Mercedes

. . . a raid on the inarticulate
with shabby equipment always deteriorating
in the general mess of imprecision of feeling. . . .

–T. S. ELIOT

Preface

WHAT DOES IT ALL MEAN?

Of the executive's five principal jobs—planning, organizing, communicating, administering, and controlling—the most pervasive and intangible remains *communicating.*

What are we really talking about? Are we talking about language, acts, performances? And as executives we ask ourselves—With whom must we communicate and how? Why is it so hard to get something across? What techniques, what knowledge, what experience, what skills needed to reach people effectively in running an organization?

We have seen great talkers who can never get anything done. We have seen strong, silent types who can. We have seen executives who write fluently and gracefully but never seem to reach anyone. We have seen executives who can scarcely write their names but seem to reach people with their short, barely legible scrawls. Why? What is it that brings home the word, the thought? What is it that galvanizes to action? *What is it*—we ask ourselves—*that as a leader, a doer, an executive, we need to know about communicating to run an organization?* That is the question this book attempts to answer.

It attempts to place the chief executive, the leader, the doer, in the various inevitable situations he will find himself in as an organization's mover and shaker. It shows him as he confronts the dilemma of choosing the level and form of communicating. It considers with him the various principal publics he must reach for himself and in behalf of his organization if he is to be effective. it considers with him how he might put together a sound communications program for his company. And finally, it faces the deepest, the most crucial, the most experiental of the arts that must be developed for true distinction and basic effectiveness—the art of thinking and the ability to listen to the future.

In collecting the material for this work and during discussion of it, I have had the aid, the knowledge, and the experience of many brilliant and distinguished men and women during my years as an executive and adviser to two great organizations. In particular, my gratitude must be expressed to Price Waterhouse & Co. and to its truly distinguished professional partners and executives for whom parts of this material were developed and tested, who graciously permitted their use here—not the least of the many generous acts of the firm.

In addition, I was fortunate enough to spend three years traveling the country, with my gifted partner, Joanne Summerfield, interviewing executives for a book entitled *Corporate Lives*, the first of a series on American life styles. Thus I was privileged to hear of the struggles of executives in this general area of communicating in an organization and to share in their efforts to reach people in their own behalf and for their companies. And this experience has led to the expansion and sometimes modification of my original jottings for this present book.

But most of all, it has been these full years of intense and enjoyable activity and the experiences themselves in each of the aspects of trying as an executive and as a person to reach others that has given this work whatever validity it may have.

GEORGE DE MARE

New York, N.Y.
January 1979

Contents

COMMUNICATING
AT THE TOP

I

STYLE

You as the writer and speaker

*Give me the right word and the right accent
and I will move the world.*
                                    —CONRAD

1

Myths and illusions about communicating . . .

"STYLE! STYLE!" FRANÇOIS FÉNELON EX-claimed, "why all writers will tell you that it is the very thing which can least of all be changed." And Isaac D'Israeli added: "After all, it is style alone by which posterity will judge of a work, for a man can have nothing truly his own but his style."

"Communications" in recent years seems to have become a fashion, a mystique, and sometimes a very strange one. Thus, before our overall view of the principles, skills, and techniques of this art, it might be worthwhile to clear up a number of myths and illusions on the subject which have become widespread. For, in the end, communicating is more a matter of style than of technique, and nothing has less served the development of effective communications or raised more misapprehensions about the nature of communicating than the enormous subordination of style to technique.

These misapprehensions about writing and communicating appear to have sprung from three main sources: first, the realization that communicating has a very strong economic function and that it can be quite complex, especially in the administration of an organization; second, an overemphasis on technique as a cure-all; and third, an impression that the communication function can somehow be shifted from the man of affairs himself to communications specialists. We see the results of such misapprehensions in a number of odd symptoms.

First, there is the sudden and tremendous concentration on communications as a business function. Grown men bow down before the awesome spectacle of the business report. Hundreds of manuals tell us how to run a business conference. Thousands of booklets inform us about the minutiae of business letters. Floods of brochures tell the executive that there is an abysmal loss of meaning between him and his associates, between him and his stockholders, between him and his employees.

Second, our communications consultants, our semanticists, our sociologists and social psychologists tell us that our slightest frown, our forgetting to say good morning, our faintest Mona Lisa smile, which may have arisen from no more than a passing heartburn, can cause cataclysmic misunderstandings, strikes in the main plant, and wholesale suicides of number two men.

Finally, in quieter tones, we are told that each man lives to some extent in a world of his own and that no event means exactly the same thing to every observer. We are informed that trying to understand another person is virtually impossible because it involves taking into account the other person's background, prejudices, and different viewpoint as well as one's own prejudices, background, and viewpoint. We are told that it involves also a profound knowledge of the language one is using and its felicities and limitations, that we must know and keep in mind the difference between a fact, an inference, an assumption, and an opinion, and that we must weigh the emotions and value judgments which our society imposes on us. In all of this, there is, of course, much truth, but the thoughtful man must place this truth in perspective.

For all of this has gone much too far. Of course, communicating is often complex and difficult. Of course, it is often wildly defective; and, of course, the dangers of misunderstanding, of mishandling language, of misusing media and channels can have and have had serious consequences. But these are the exceptions. What has been overlooked is the tremendous success of the great bulk of our communicating efforts. What has been underestimated is the truly marvelous power and effectiveness of our principal means of communications, our language. And, finally, what has been disregarded in these head-shakings is the ability of the intelligent, thoughtful man to handle the art quite successfully in important moments, to master the various skills and techniques without enormous plunges into the deeps, and to meet his communications needs in almost all the situations in life and in the world of affairs which are of true consequence by putting his own style and fervor into what he has to say.

The anxieties arising from this overemphasis on the difficulties and complexity of communications, the misdirection of attention which the overemphasis on technique as a cure-all has brought about, and the overreliance on specialists have resulted, the author believes, in seven myths and illusions which are widespread, which we may glance at here, and which should perhaps be laid to rest. We can then go on to the more serious overall view of what is really needed to gain a mastery of the art.

*M*YTH NO. 1: COMMUNICATING IS A DIFFICULT AND COMPLEX ART RESERVED TO THE COMMUNICATIONS EXPERT

Let us be in the minority here. Let us not consider communicating either difficult or complex. Let us not be impressed either by the long dissertations on the great loss of meaning between sender and receiver, the great barriers between people with different experiences and emotional sets, the profound problems in making clear business' complex situations and problems.

If a man has lived as a human being among others, he will have had some twenty to sixty years of practice in the art of communications and will generally have proved himself to be quite adequate at it. The kind of communicating called for in the world of affairs is often, in the author's opinion, of a far simpler type than that called for, say, in a large family, a prep school, college, or most of life's key situations, and the use of common sense and the skills derived from these situations plus all this experience, if a man of goodwill is reasonably intelligent, should make communicating in business comparatively simple for him.

There are two provisos. First, a man must like what he is doing. If he does not, he will communicate that dislike, and this will ruin any sympathetic reception to the substance of his communications.

Second, he must be reasonably intelligent. Half the problems ascribed to lack of ability to communicate arise from stupidity. If a man is, shall we say, an idiot, then people will tend to be kind to him and say that he has a communicating problem, which, of course, is true. They will then send him to a communications consultant, and the communications consultant will not be able to help him, and they will then say the consultant is an idiot or that he also has a communicating problem.

*M*YTH NO. 2:
WRITING WELL IS A DIFFICULT AND COMPLEX ART

The ability to write well in the great majority of men is a matter of practice and cultivation. It is not a matter of being born with special skills because no one is born with any skill as complex as writing. In another sense, however, all human beings are born with the natural inclination to express themselves in language. As the song goes: "Fish got to swim and birds got to fly." And through the operations of their culture, human beings got to express themselves in language or they stop growing and deteriorate.

The ability to write develops early in a human being; and, if not impeded by bad teaching and bad experiences and if promoted by practice, it develops rapidly into a major skill. But it must be practiced hard and often. Let us put it in its simplest form. A man who has written 10,000 words will be a better writer than a man who has written 5,000 words. A man who has written 50,000 words will be a better writer than one who has written 10,000 words, and a man who has written a million words will be a better writer than one who has written 50,000 words. That is the long and short of it.

We admit genius. We even admit unusual talent—there is Shakespeare and there is Hemingway, but that is as far as we should go. If a man wants to be a good writer, let him write.

MYTH NO. 3:
THERE IS A RIGHT WAY AND A WRONG WAY TO COMMUNICATE MATERIAL

Unless one wants to admit at the outset that the rightness of a piece of communications has a direct correlation with a man's position in life, this "either/or" approach is one of the most distressing of our communicating myths. It is one with Flaubert's *le mot juste*, the exact word, and it has sent thousands into hopeless convulsions trying to find that needle in the haystack of language, that white camellia blossom in the dark well.

There are a dozen, a hundred, perhaps a thousand ways to communicate material well and the same or even an infinite number of ways to communicate it badly. Try to pick one of the many right ways. Most of the time, if a man is reasonably intelligent and aware of the current forms and techniques, his way is best on any job for which he is responsible. It is best to do it your own way. It is almost always a mistake to try to second-guess the way someone else would do it.

MYTH NO. 4:
STEREOTYPES AND CLICHES SHOULD BE AVOIDED

Quite the contrary. Usually, a phrase, a pattern, an expression, or a form becomes a stereotype or a cliché because it is so good it has been overworked. I would have men learn all stereotypes and clichés, learn them well, and learn how and when to use them. When the man himself comes up with something brilliant, original, and fresh, everyone else will use it, and it will then become a cliché, a stereotype.

We study books of models. Many of these models have become stereotypes, of course, because they are the best there are. When we have learned them, however, we are then ready to go on to make original contributions ourselves.

So let us know our clichés and stereotypes. Let us treasure them. They will stand us in good stead in many a situation when our own brains have given out.

*M*YTH NO. 5:
A GOOD WRITER KNOWS HOW TO USE WORDS

Actually, good writers are good at handling *material* of certain types, not necessarily words. Theodore Dreiser was a major novelist, but he had a tin ear for words, for language. James Farrell, who wrote the *Studs Lonigan* series, did a beautiful job of making alive the experiences of growing up in the Chicago Irish community, but he writes, as someone said, "as if he were wearing mittens." Faulkner, God love him, was (at least in the author's opinion) an atrocious writer if measured by his tortured language, and Proust has some beautiful, lingering language, but it would never pass the Flesch readability test.

What a good writer has is the ability to handle material of specific kinds and to do so with conspicuous depth and flair. His medium is language as a sculptor's medium is stone, but he is not an English teacher and he need not be drummed out of the corps for a split infinitive.

What is the point? The point is that as men of affairs, it would seem that our job in communications is to handle the material we are dealing with thoughtfully, in perspective and with flair, and in the beginning to let the words fall where they may. As we gain in practice and experience, our words will fall better and better, but the material and our organizing and handling of it is the thing.

*M*YTH NO. 6:
YOU SHOULD THINK OUT WHAT YOU WANT TO SAY BEFORE YOU COMMIT IT TO PAPER

Again, this myth has been repeated over and over, and again quite the contrary. Very few men can formulate mentally what must be said if the message is at all complex or the circumstances at all new. What they need is to see all the elements and "work out" what they want to say. How does one know what one really wants to say except in the vaguest sense until one has worked it out? The answer is really that a man does not and cannot. Meanings and effective meanings are worked out, sometimes laboriously. Even when the meaning may seem clear, the way of expressing it may require a lot of pencil work and experimentation. Usually, a good message "emerges"; it is not formulated. Some of the shallowest, least effective communications are those "thought out" off the top of the head without careful pencil work.

So as a first step, it might be suggested that we commit everything to paper and then start working out what we want to say. Too many executives pride themselves on being able to formulate their thoughts before committing them to paper. Usually, this can be done only when what the executive has to say has been said by him many times before and he is actually simply repeating a formula.

We should not be afraid to get down and dig, to put it all on paper. That way we clarify our problem. We see all the elements. We have something to push around and work with; we develop an approach—and, behold, maybe we will be able to say what we have to say with true distinction.

*M*YTH NO. 7:
YOU SHOULD SAY WHAT YOU MEAN

If most of us in business took a special pride in saying what we meant, we would quite often deservedly be out of a job. The purpose of most business communications is to be helpful, to get things done, not to express ourselves. The question to ask about a business communication or almost any communication is: *What is its value?* If the answer is none, forget it. Business has its own ceremonies and locutions which serve a social or sociological purpose of cementing friendships and good relationships, of helping make the commercial life enjoyable, fruitful, or at the least bearable. "Ceremony," John Selden wrote, "keeps up all things. 'Tis like a penny glass to a rich spirit or some excellent water. Without it, the water were spilt, the spirit lost."

In some fields, we use a soothing and dignifying

language—and, of course, a ridiculous one. No one is ever paid; he is "compensated" or "remunerated." He is not promoted; he "takes on broader responsibilities." He is not demoted; "his special qualifications make him invaluable in a new assignment." And he is never fired; he is "allowed to find himself in something more suited to his interests."

And that is as it should be.

Let us say what we mean, if we must, to our wife or our best friend (though I do not necessarily advocate this either) but observe the ceremonies in business. There is a difference between observing a convention and communicating, and many a rising executive, feeling his integrity debauched by what he conceives of as the hypocritical response, confuses the two. A retirement speech is not a form of communications. One is not an oath to tell the assembled multitude with what a sigh of relief it is that old Bumbling Bill is finally bowing out. A Christmas greeting is not a communication. It is a ceremony. The author remembers well the annual crisis in a big corporation with which he was associated over the president's Christmas message to the stockholders. Every year, beginning with the Executive Vice President and on down, we would take a crack at it. Our best talents would work on it, and the message would be hammered out, word by painful word, phrase by tortured phrase, until we had what we thought was a foolproof message. You have seen the kind. It had been a good year, the message would say, or, if it had been a bad year, we called it "a year fraught with challenge," and the president would like to express to each and every one of us, and so on . . .

Yet when we were done, there always seemed to be something lacking, until one year, after our high-priced talent had done its painful best, one of the assistants in the author's group, a moderately talented, high-spirited chap in his late twenties, scrawled across the bottom of a second proof: *Why doesn't the bastard just say Merry Christmas?*

Of course. So much for ceremonials.

There are times, obviously, when telling off the boss, preparing the harsh communication, or laying it on the line is beneficial and necessary both to the recipient and to the business. At these times, if one has any integrity, he will do so.

Lincoln's famous remark must always be remembered: "To sin by silence when they should protest makes cowards of men." But be sure what you say has relevance. The question should always be with a business communication, not are you saying what you mean, but *does what you are saying have any value?*

THE OVERALL VIEW

So let us lay to rest these seven myths about writing and communicating. Most people in business and the world of affairs are not good writers because they do not write enough. They are not very good at communicating because they are not dealing with the material they have to offer with care and integrity. They do not bring to their communications their years of experience as human beings in life's important situations. They do not make sufficient effort or take sufficient pride in organizing and handling the material they have to offer. And sometimes they appear to believe that communicating in business or the world of affairs is of a different order and kind from communicating in life. Such, it must be emphasized, is not the case.

Thus, in this work, we shall take the overall view. We shall study first how to give sparkle to our language. We shall undertake to find our way through the jungle of business communications. We shall consider how to reach the major "publics" of an organization. We shall consider how to get substance into our communications, and finally we shall look at what the sociologists and social psychologists have to tell us about communications and about the art of communicating as a whole. This work is filled with material "everybody knows," but it is also filled with the experience of seeing how the executive, the business leader fails to use this knowledge and fails to use it at his peril.

2

You as the writer: how to bring your writing to life

"LANGUAGE," MARK HOPKINS WROTE, "IS THE picture and counterpart of thought." "Style," Henri-Frédéric Amiel added, "is what gives thought value and currency." Thus, the most fundamental category of technique required in the art of communicating is the skill in the use of language, written and oral. Lord Moran in his memoirs on Winston Churchill wrote in *The Diaries of Lord Moran:*

> Few men have stuck so religiously to one craft—the handling of words. In peace it made his political fortune, in war it has won all men's hearts. "It all began at Harrow," he said. Sitting at the bottom of the school, under something of a cloud, he discovered that he could do what other boys could not do—he could write. From the beginning "personal distinction" was his goal; above all he wanted to be an orator. He read everything he could get hold of about Lord Chatham, the great eighteenth-century orator; he studied his father's speeches; he practiced his own before the looking glass.

"Personal distinction" was the goal, and the means was language. The collection of dicta and suggestions put together in this and the succeeding chapter is in effect, therefore, a collection of professional approaches which can help the man of affairs to bring his writing to life and to put sparkle in his talks, and these are the first and most basic of his needs in this attempt to master the art of reaching others.

No instructions or hints, of course, will in themselves give effect to these approaches any more than (on a simpler plane) reading an instruction manual will teach a man how to swim. One must first plunge into the water and become accustomed to the medium. So only practice and cultivation will make a man an accomplished writer and speaker. The sheer bulk of writing or speaking he undertakes will have a lot to do with it. If a man writes a great deal, he is apt to become a good writer. If he speaks a great deal, he is apt to become a good speaker. If he does neither, he is guaranteed not to become either. That is the crux of it.

All forms of communication in our world of affairs presuppose substance, that is, something to be communicated. These notes on the arts of writing and speaking deal with the developing, organizing, and handling of that substance through language. Again, the value of the communication depends largely on the quality of the message, and the effectiveness of the communication depends on the perceived value of the message to the recipient.

The section on writing which follows includes the basic techniques of getting started, collecting or developing the substance, organizing the material, the characteristics of good writing, and a case study of one of the forms with which the business leader should be familiar, as well as a summarized twenty-five hints that can give sparkle to your writing. This chapter and the chapter on speaking have been stripped of everything but fundamentals. They are approaches which have been effective and are summaries of the more basic writing and speaking techniques.

A SIMPLIFIED APPROACH TO WRITING

Getting started

Many men of affairs can never become good writers for a very simple reason. They can never get started writing. They are afraid. They are appalled at their own clumsiness with words. They are discouraged because they cannot live up to the standards of self-expression they expect of themselves.

There is a simple cure for this kind of fear. It has nothing to do with grammar or usage, those ground rules of writing and speaking, important as they may be. It is far more basic. It is simply: Have something to say. Lose yourself in your subject.

Let us speak directly to the business executive here.

The mind has two major faculties—its creative faculty and its critical faculty. It cannot use both successfully at the same time. Your own mind has probably been trained largely in the critical and analytical faculties. You learned your grammar well. You know the rules of composition. You can spell. Still you cannot write or speak with any ease or effectiveness. Why? The answer is that you are trying to write with your critical faculty. The critical faculty insists that whatever emerges from your pen or typewriter be "perfect." It criticizes everything your creative mind is able to grind out. Under these circumstances, your creative mind quits. You become sterile.

In getting started, therefore, let your critical faculties lie dormant. Forget about rules, grammar, and diction. Your object at this stage is to produce, to get it out in any way you can. Immerse yourself in your subject, grab any sort of language you have at your command, and pour it out.

There will be plenty of time later to use your critical faculties, to check your vocabulary and grammar, and to consult someone more skilled than you for specific pointers on your writing when you come to revise. For revise you must. One professional aphorism is: *An article is never written; it is rewritten*—a good rule for all written material. So with the first draft, have no fear.

1. Get your material out in the form of a rough draft.

2. Use whatever language and form come easily to you.

3. Realize that this is the first draft and no one will see it, much less shoot you for it.

Collecting material

The secret of good writing is good material. No one should approach a subject without informing himself of what has already been done in the field. This is elementary, but it is remarkable how often the principle is overlooked. The professional writer—the informed man, in fact—always knows what has been written on his subject and the way it has been written. He goes on from there. The consequences of not having read what has been written on your subject may be not only an unfortunate repetition of what has been done and perhaps done better, but also an overlooking of material essential to the informed handling of your topic. You can find this published material in the library. It is the first major source of the substance of any piece.

The second is experience.

Experience—yours or that of others you have known or know in the field—will provide freshness, sparkle, and life to your article. It will be that part of the substance of your piece that is "original." It will be considered by your readers as the most valuable portion—the reason for being of your presentation. Therefore, you must dig into yourself carefully for this kind of material. And, second, you must collect from your colleagues and the experts in this field. That is an essential part of original research.

Good writing, then, stems first from good material. Material is of two kinds:

1. Published work on the subject and in the field.

2. Experience—your own or that of others who are authorities in the field.

Sources of this material are:

1. The library.

2. Your own experience and that of your colleagues (mostly in the form of anecdotes, case histories, and the like). If you ask for experiences from your colleagues, ask specific questions that will elicit specific material. The value of such original material lies partly in its concreteness and immediacy.

Giving it structure

Good writing depends not only on good material, but also on good organization. In effect, good thinking makes good writing. If you know exactly what you want to say, if you have defined the boundaries of what you wish to communicate, you are in a position to organize your material effectively. Badly organized material does not communicate its burden of thought directly enough to the reader. It confuses him. It wastes his time.

So it is that the experienced executive "puts together" his material in a simple, logical manner. He makes his point directly and completely, and all his material moves toward making that point. Here is a simple way in which to organize material.

You place before you all the material you have gathered for your presentation. You sketch a rough outline of what you wish to communicate. The outline need not be detailed. It is meant only as a general guide for the placing of material. Then you place your material in the form of notes, case histories, examples, and verbal illustrations within the framework of your rough outline.

A draft written in this way will have "organization." It will not, of course, have perfect organization. You will have to work on the rough edges, discard some material, find other material to fill blanks in your structure. When you have finished polishing and fitting in the relevant material you have been able to gather, your presentation should make its point simply, fully, and with a wealth of example. Your rough outline is the device which should hold everything together.

Characteristics of good writing

The finest material and organization may be wasted unless the work is presented in effective prose. Five characteristics will immediately occur to you in handling your presentation. They are (1) tone, (2) completeness, (3) conciseness, (4) concreteness, and (5) readability.

Tone is of great importance in communication, since you are dealing with people. The tone in which you cast your letter or memorandum or report is an index to those who read it of your poise, of the quality of your personality, and even to some extent of your authority in your subject. A courteous, pleasant tone and a tempo that meets the requirements of the field in which you are working are important elements in achieving a cordial reception for what you have to say. Completeness and conciseness require no explanation. As a seventeenth-century verse puts it:

> The written word should be clean as bone
> Clear as light
> Firm as stone
> Two words are not
> As good as one

and Sydney Smith advised: "Run your pen through every other word you have written. You have no idea what vigor it will give your style."

The fourth characteristic of good written work—concreteness—requires, however, some further discussion. It has a special meaning as used in the communications of the business leader. It means simply the number, variety, and aptness of the examples, case histories, or illustrations that form the body of your piece. Whether it be a business letter, a special report, or a memorandum, the use of example will give weight and color to your subject. In longer forms of writing, its use becomes of prime importance. Give your work the "concreteness" of example and illustration.

The fifth characteristic of good writing with which we shall deal is readability. Style, of course, requires something more than mere readability, but without readability there is no communication.

Taken as a class, corporate and professional writing, particularly in the areas where it counts most—in stockholders' reports, for example, and in essential communications with employees—is within the reading grasp of only six out of one hundred American adults. This is not because the ideas are hard to understand. It is simply because the writing is not readable. Those who write the reports or the instructions may know their subjects, but they have not learned basic word skills. They do not know how to communicate. They cannot write simple, readable English.

Readability does not, as you might suppose, depend on the complexity of the thoughts involved. It depends primarily on the way in which these thoughts are presented. Very simple ideas may be presented in an unreadable manner, and quite complex ideas in a very readable manner. Take this statement:

> An increase in an employee's rate of pay will not become effective prior to the date on which the employee has completed a minimum of 13 weeks' actual work at his regular occupational classification.

That is bad writing and hard reading. It wastes the reader's time. It may be important to him so he will have to puzzle it out, but it could have been written this way:

> An employee must work at least 13 weeks at his regular job before he can receive an increase in pay.

This version will at least communicate, and that is the basic job of writing.

Given a sound, well-organized piece, how, then, do I put it in readable prose? How do I get "readability"? The answer is now well known and easier than you may think.

What makes "readability"?

Well, a number of elements, but three are of overriding importance. They are (1) short sentences, (2) few syllables or affixes per hundred words, and (3) frequent personal references per hundred words.

A number of formulas have been devised to help test the readability of writing. Perhaps the best known of these is that of Rudolph Flesch in his book, *The Art of Plain Talk*. Here it is.

Take the average number of affixes per hundred words in your writing. An affix is an addition to a root word (prefixes are added in front, suffixes in back; both are called affixes). Subtract the average number of personal references in that hundred words. A personal reference is a proper name or a pronoun. Divide by two. Then add the average number of words per sentence. Check the result against this scale:

Readability scale

0 to 13	Very Easy	36 to 43	Fairly Difficult
13 to 20	Easy	43 to 52	Difficult
20 to 29	Fairly Easy	52 and above	Unreadable
29 to 36	Standard		

Example. Let us take this passage from Thomas Mann's short story *Death in Venice* and analyze it for readability.

This life in the bonds of art, had not he himself, in the days of his youth and in the very spirit of those bourgeois forefathers, pronounced mocking judgment on it? And yet at bottom it had been so like their own! It had been a service, and he a soldier, like some of them. And art was war—a grilling, exhausting struggle that nowadays wore one out before one could grow old. It had been a life of self-conquest, a life against odds, dour, steadfast, abstinent. He had made it symbolical of the kind of overstrained heroism the time admired, and he was entitled to call it manly, even courageous.

There are 111 words in this passage, a little over the 100-word sample usually used, but no matter. The underlined syllables are affixes. There are 26 affixes. The double-underlined words are personal references. There are 9 personal references. The passage has 6 sentences, with an *average* word count of 18½ words per sentence.

Using the formula, we take the number of affixes in the passage, 26; subtract the number of personal references, 9; and divide by 2: $26 - 9 = 17 \div 2 = 8\frac{1}{2}$. Then we add the average number of words per sentence, 18½, and we have the number 27. On the Readability Scale, 27 is Fairly Easy.

Thomas Mann's ideas in his masterpiece may be complex and subtle, but his writing is quite readable. Now try the yardstick on the last business article or report you read. And then try the yardstick on several typical examples of your own writing.

What, then, we ask again, makes writing readable? Basically, readable writing must have (1) short sentences, (2) few affixes, and (3) many personal references. This is, of course, a simplification. To make business writing more readable, chop up those long sentences. Vary the length of your sentences, of course, but keep the average short. Second, avoid those long, many-syllabled, Latinized words. Instead of saying *assistance,* say *help.* Instead of saying *the employment of,* say *the use of;* instead of saying *inasmuch as,* say *since.* And then use, wherever possible, personal references. In "professionalese," that odd sort of professional writing which has grown up in the business world as well as in most of the professions, there is a deadly fear of intruding the personal note. Almost every sentence is in the passive voice, and every remark is anonymously stated. People like to fasten on the source of a remark or an action. They will drown in a sea of unreferred acts and thoughts. Write with the informality with which you speak and you will have more readers.

Here are a few more details. Use many verbs, few adjectives. Avoid the frequent use of "empty" phrases, such as, *with regard to* for *about; prior to* for *before;* and *in the event that* for *if.* Avoid *moreovers* and *furthermores*—they are usually unnecessary. Do not try to fill your sentences too full. Keep one thought to a sentence. Use the language of people.

Yes, in business, we have been guilty, indeed, of what has been called "that invisible empire of word deathtraps" and "that great Slow-Down Wall of doubletalk." We are not the only ones. Let us look at Stuart Chase's famous example of the plumber who wrote to the Bureau of Standards saying that he had found hydrochloric acid fine for cleaning drains, and was it harmless? Washington replied: "The efficacy of hydrochloric acid is indisputable, but the chlorine residue is incompatible with metallic permanence."

The plumber wrote back that he was mighty glad the Bureau agreed with him. The Bureau replied with a note of alarm: "We cannot assume responsibility for the production of toxic and noxious residues with hydrochloric acid, and suggest that you use an alternate procedure." The plumber was happy to learn that the Bureau still agreed with him.

Whereupon Washington exploded: "Don't use hydrochloric acid; it eats hell out of pipes!"

And, as a last example of noncommunicating writing, here is a legal definition that the government put out:

> Ultimate consumer means a person or group of persons, generally constituting a domestic household, who purchase eggs generally at the individual stores of retailers or

purchase and receive deliveries of eggs at the place of abode of the individual or domestic household from producers or retail route sellers and who use such eggs for their consumption as food.

What does this mean? Why, it's simple: Ultimate consumers are people who buy eggs to eat them. That's all.

You owe it to yourself and to your readers to write readable prose.

*T*WENTY-FIVE TIPS THAT CAN GIVE SPARKLE TO YOUR WRITING

1. Show, don't tell. Use examples, case histories, verbal illustrations, etc. Avoid philosophizing or lengthy, unrelieved explanations.

2. Be specific. Use the word that brings a picture to mind.

3. Vary the length and construction of both sentences and paragraphs. Avoid excessive use of the passive voice, common in "professionalese."

4. Write as you would talk to a friend—simply, clearly, without flourish and affectation.

5. Never let a first draft out of your hands. Good work is not written; it is rewritten.

6. Shun unnecessary adjectives and adverbs to simplify your writing. Avoid qualifiers such as *nearly* and *almost*—they kill the force of your sentence. Do not use the adverb *very*. Be specific, never vague. Don't say "several men appeared"; make up your mind—three? four?

7. Words are thoughts. To catch meanings, you need a net of words. What you can express in words, you know. The rest you only feel. Build your "use" vocabulary. It will bring you a greater control of meaning. All intelligence tests are mainly based on size of vocabulary. Learn new words, new meanings. Use them constantly.

8. Keep a notebook for colorful words and phrases and well-expressed thoughts that you meet in your reading.

This is the secret of the professional writer's polish, variety, and felicity with language.

9. Use analogy and "comparing" symbols. They add color to your writing.

10. Start in the middle. This is an old fiction writer's adage. Avoid long introductions. Catch the reader immediately. Go immediately to the heart of the matter.

11. Cultivate the tone of your work. A courteous, gracious tone is like a pleasant, attractive appearance. It wins acceptance for what you have to say.

12. Research your subject thoroughly. This means that you should read or skim through the principal books of the subject and the latest articles on it.

13. Look into yourself for all personal experiences that have to do with your subject. This is the "new" material which you can provide that no one else can give. That is what your reader will read for.

14. Write letters to other experts on your subject asking them specifically for their experiences to illuminate specific points in your report or article.

15. Interview colleagues, if possible. Valuable material is acquired in this way.

16. Results of questionnaires properly made up and sent to carefully selected lists form extremely valuable material. The purpose of the questionnaire must be persuasively indicated. The questionnaire must be brief, well phrased, and specific.

17. Take notes first on your reading and, second, on what you remember of interviews and talks with colleagues. Make rough outlines of the content of your report or article. Place the notes and material from letters and questionnaires in the order in which you wish to use them in your work.

18. Allow yourself a brooding period of from two days to a week to mull over the material you have received and have at hand. This incubating period is essential so that your subconscious mind can assimilate your material. Rest before you embark on a presentation.

Think of something else. When you have brooded and rested a few days, then sit down and write it off.

19. When you have roughed out a first draft, allow it to cool for at least a day. You need a time span to secure perspective on what you have done.

20. Revise. At least one revision and polishing is necessary. Except in rare cases, even the experienced professional revises.

21. As you write, be natural. Avoid a portentous, self-important, officialese cast to your style.

22. Watch your grammar, your usage, the purity of your language. Choose the right form of the word. Note the difference in usage between "shall" and "will," "lie" and "lay," "implication" and "inference," and others.

23. Don't be afraid of language, words. Skill in their use comes from practice, experimentation. The English language is the world's most powerful instrument. It is spoken and understood by more people than any other language in the world. It has the largest vocabulary of any language on earth. Use it. Cherish it. Be understood in it.

24. Test your writing constantly for readability.

25. Read. Read. Read. Principally books. It doesn't matter so much at first what you read as that you acquire the "reading habit." Then read widely. Apart from all its other benefits in life-experiences gained, reading gives a man a great advantage in self-expression. It adds depth and polish to his writing and speech.

3

You as the speaker: a guide to successful talks
...

"SURELY WHOEVER SPEAKS TO ME IN THE RIGHT voice, him or her I shall follow." So wrote Walt Whitman, and so it has been for men.

Like the art of writing, the art of speaking is one of the basic skills required in communicating. Also, like writing, it is one which demands a lifetime of cultivation and development. "Speeches are veritable transactions in the human commonwealth," Hegel said, "in fact, very gravely influential transactions." And Rufus Choate wrote: "It is the peculiarity of some schools of eloquence that they embody and utter, not merely the individual genius and character of the speaker, but a national consciousness—a national era, a mood, a hope, a dread, a despair—in which you listen to the spoken history of the time."

Very few of the talks given will embody "the spoken history of the time," but the man of affairs must be prepared to acquit himself well as a speaker before his peers. And he must be prepared to have substance in whatever he says. The greatest crime a speaker can commit, in this author's opinion, is to speak when he has nothing to say, and this is perhaps the reigning social crime of our times. As the witty Thomas B. Reed, Speaker of the House, once remarked about his colleagues: "They never open their mouths without subtracting from the sum of human knowledge."

Presentation and technique are secondary. From the half a hundred works on techniques of speaking before groups, the notes which follow distill out the simplest and the most basic approaches to bring life to an executive's talks. Yet no rule, only substance—the amount of illustration, example, original thinking, and vital knowledge—will make these techniques work. And what substance is germane? "Every investigation that can be made as regards those duties for which an orator should be held responsible," Demosthenes said, "I bid you make. And what are those duties? To discern events in their beginnings, to foresee what is coming, and to forewarn others." Modern life and the world of affairs have added a few other subjects with which we intend to deal later, but to the thoughtful business leader, it is not only the ceremonies of speech for which he must make himself responsible but mainly the substance.

The techniques of presentation which follow, therefore, presuppose substance. These techniques are again stripped down and made as simple as possible and are dealt with under preparation, pattern, appearance, and delivery. They may be familiar, but it is important to review them.

A SIMPLIFIED SPEECH PRESENTATION

Preparation

The modern speech, like the article, is built around the "angle" or theme or unifying idea. Strictly speaking, there are two types of engagements, and they require distinctly different techniques. One is summed up in the term "delivering a paper." The other is described as "giving a talk." In the first, you will be reading from a prepared paper. In the second, you will be speaking from notes or, if possible, without notes.

In each case, you prepare your speech by finding the theme. And you build your whole speech around this theme.

Let us take first the speech that is put on paper and then read from the paper. Preparation of this type of speech is much like the preparation of the modern article. It involves (1) finding the angle, (2) securing the basic material, (3) securing the "original" material, (4) making a rough outline of the speech, and finally (5) writing it.

In preparing the speech, however, there is one important additional consideration involved—how does it sound when read aloud? A piece to be read and a piece to be heard possess very different basic requirements. One may present the writer's style; the other must present his personality. The reader can go back and reread a passage; the listener must get the point immediately—he cannot, so to speak, rerun the sound track.

That is why when writing a speech to be read aloud, you must build into it enough varied repetition of the theme or angle to keep the hearer at all times aware of your main thesis and to give the speech unity. In the words of the old preacher: "You tells 'em what you's gonna tell 'em; you tells 'em; den you tells 'em you tol' 'em."

Second, you write the speech to be read aloud in a "conversational" manner—that is, a manner that fits your particular way of speaking. It is always well to write with the easy informality of speech, but here the easy informality of speech must, in fact, be your particular form of speaking. It must possess your rhythms, tempo, and characteristic word patterns. The sentences must be of the type that are natural for you to voice, the words easy for you to pronounce and use.

Readers of professional papers, in particular, are prone to stupefy their audience with a "literary" type of presentation rather than a natural, "easily talked" paper. It is important to get this "talkability" into a paper that must be read aloud, and perhaps the best way is to read it aloud several times and make changes in sentence structure and wording to conform to your delivery.

Working out a pattern

We offer here a simple pattern* which has been found useful to speakers in preparing a speech, whether it be a paper to be read or a talk from notes.

*Formula developed by Richard C. Borden in *Public Speaking—As Listeners Like It.* Copyright 1935 by Harper & Row; renewed 1963 by Richard C. Borden. Reprinted by permission of the author and Harper & Row.

This pattern is encompassed in four key idea-phrases: (1) the *Ho Hum Crasher,* (2) *Why Bring That Up?* (3) *For Instance* . . ., and (4) *So What?*

Ho hum crasher. This is the beginning of the speech. It is important here to say something that will seize your audience's interest immediately, will wake them up, will get them with you. This is just as valid for the man who reads a paper before a professional society as it is for the so-called "popular" speaker, who speaks from notes or extemporaneously. You have three or four seconds in which to make your first impression on your listeners; then, even though they may be "condemned" to listen to you, if you have not said something interesting, provocative, even startling, you will find it difficult to get them back with you for the rest of your talk. The classic example of the Ho Hum Crasher is the opening sentence of the speaker who was asked to talk on traffic accidents before a large audience. He began: "Gentlemen, one of you will not reach home tonight."

Why bring that up? Having captured your audience with the Ho Hum Crasher, you must now give them the reason for your startling or interesting observation. The reason is the subject of your speech. After the foregoing Ho Hum Crasher, the speaker might explain that one out of so many people in that town is injured or killed in an automobile accident every twenty-four hours. So the chances are that someone in that very audience will not get home safely that night. Now he intends to talk about these traffic fatalities. That is why he made that remark. That is the subject for the evening.

For instance . . . "All right, give us an example!" That is the constant cry of every audience. That is the heart of your talk. Here you marshal the case histories, the examples, the anecdotes, the verbal illustrations that make up the substance of your speech. In general, a talk is impressive in direct proportion to the vividness, aptness, and freshness of the examples and case histories provided. Particulars stay in the mind; generalities fade. Make no statement without a "For instance . . ." Good examples and good case histories are hard to come by, but they "make" the speech, as they "make" the article. Here, according to the tone of your speech, your case histories and examples should be well told, carefully expressed. They may be humorous, when the subject permits; grave, when appropriate. When humor is used, it must be in key and apt. It must make a point in the context of your subject. And when all your examples and case histories—your "for instances"—have been presented, the range of the speech's subject matter should have been covered. And now—

So what? this is the conclusion. This is the reason you delivered that paper or gave that talk. This answers the question: "Why am I telling you all this?" It requires that the audience feel that an adequate point has been made by your paper or your talk, that their time spent listening to you was worthwhile. The "So what?" can range from the conclusion in a paper before a learned society that this new method presented may open new fields of research to the exhortation to install traffic lights and review drivers licenses in that town to cut down the spate of traffic fatalities.

The four key phrases, then, can help build a speech so that it "moves" and has force. Remember them: the *Ho Hum Crasher, Why Bring That Up?, For Instance . . ., So What?*

How do you come on?

Your appearance before an audience in itself does much to insure the success of your talk. The word "appearance" used here means not only how you are dressed and groomed but also your manner as you stand before the hearers, as you look at them, even in such preliminaries as how you approach the front of the platform.

The first job of the inexperienced speaker is to strip away mannerisms. You have seen them in others. A man, well dressed, properly groomed, fine appearance, steps out on the platform. Then it begins. His subject is interesting. He speaks well. But you cannot concentrate on what he is saying. He cannot stand still. He cannot just be quietly relaxed. He is a nose-puller. He rocks back and forth on his heels. He scratches his head. He distracts the attention of his audience with these nervous and largely unconscious mannerisms, and thereby spoils a good speech.

So strip away your mannerisms. Avoid distracting moves and gestures. Don't pour a glass of water in front of your audience. Don't look at your watch. Don't make gestures that take your audience from what you are saying.

Second, face the audience with confidence. This is not difficult if you realize that they are there because they respect you and are eager to hear what you have to say. Never apologize. Apologizing emphasizes defects. If you are an inexperienced speaker, if your subject seems weak, if somebody has stolen your fire, the audience will know it soon enough— don't emphasize it by apologizing. You owe it to your audience to keep them interested and absorbed. At any rate, if you are doing your best, what have you to apologize for?

Can you learn to have the right touch?

The quality of a man's delivery depends to a great degree on practice. We are using the word "delivery" here to cover the actual speaking itself—the manner in which you say what you have to say. Delivery includes tone, voice inflections, loudness, and tempo. And it further means all these in relation to your subject matter. None of these qualities of a good delivery can be achieved mechanically without relationship to your subject and your audience. But they are qualities you must know about.

First: *loudness*. How loudly should you speak? There is much talk about breath control and speaking from the abdomen. The point is you must speak loudly enough so that the man in the last row can hear. And that means speaking, not shouting. It means that you must look out over your audience and wing your voice to each and every listener. It is futile, of course, to have prepared a good speech and then not deliver it loudly enough for sections of the audience to hear it.

Second: *inflection*. Vary the pitch and tone of your voice. A monotonous voice will either irritate or put the audience to sleep. If you are thinking what you are saying, you will make the proper intonations. Avoid either monotony of voice or sing-song effect. If you speak "naturally," that is, with the animation and verve that you would display in telling a

friend something interesting and important, you will generally achieve a natural inflection. Your tones will ring true.

Third: *tempo.* Timing is not just something you are born
with; it is a quality you can develop. And it comes largely
from a sensitivity to the moods and responses of your audience. Objectively, tempo means the speed and rhythm with
which you speak. It means also knowing when to be silent.
When an audience is laughing at one of your sallies, don't try
to talk through their laughter. When you are pointing to material you wish them to look at, be silent and let them look.
They cannot listen to you and look at the same time unless
you are merely reading what is said on the chart. Tempo is
the speed of your speech also. Talk fast enough to keep your
audience interested, but not so fast that the listener cannot
follow you. You must know when to emphasize, when to raise
your voice, when to lower it.

But most of all, there is the "feel" of the audience. You
are speaking to people—that is the thing you must never
forget. You must feel their moods just as you feel the moods of
a good friend. Forget, if you will, loudness, inflection, and
timing. If you have rapport with the audience, these will take
care of themselves. Speak always with a sense that you are
talking to someone. Never "lose" him or them. And cease
when you have had your say or you sense that your audience
has responded to the full.

One last word on delivery: you must give of yourself. The
best material in the world cannot reach the hearers of a
speech except through you. And the audience wants something else with it—it wants you. It wants to feel your own
sincerity and absorption in your subject, and it wants that
"lift" which energy, vitality, and a bestowing of oneself give.

*F*OLKLORE OF SPEAKING:
TWENTY-FIVE TIPS THAT CAN ADD QUALITY
TO YOUR TALKS

1. In preparing a talk, remember "tone." An agreeable
   tone is as important as good subject matter.

2. Pattern your speech along the four key idea-phrases:
   (1) the *Ho Hum Crasher* to wake up your audience and

get it with you, (2) *Why Bring That Up?* to emphasize your talk's relevance, timeliness, and importance to that audience, (3) *For Instance* . . . to give your talk color and body, and (4) *So What?* to conclude with the theme or significance of the talk to those listening.

3. Speak loudly enough to be heard in the back rows.

4. Watch troublesome mannerisms. Don't be a head-scratcher, nose-rubber, key-jingler. Strip yourself of annoying habits on the platform and learn to stand quietly and naturally.

5. Do not apologize for anything. Just do your best.

6. Face your audience with confidence. You would not have been asked to speak if they did not respect you and want to hear you.

7. If you read a paper, look up at your audience constantly. Don't bury yourself in the paper; keep a grip on your hearers.

8. Vary your tone, loudness, and tempo. Don't be monotonous or singsong. These variations will come naturally to the subject matter if you speak with spirit.

9. Fill your speech with stories, anecdotes, case histories, and examples. They are the lifeblood of a good talk.

10. Use your own language—the language that comes naturally to you. If you are reading from a written speech, be sure the piece is couched in the language that is natural to you, that it "talks" well.

11. Dress to suit your audience. Usually, dark suit and white shirt are best. See that buttons are sewed on. Leave your audience with nothing but your speech to think about.

12. Give your talk unity. Tell them what you are going to tell them; tell them; tell them you told them.

13. Again: Show, don't just tell. You can tell the same thing a dozen times if you tell it through the medium of a dozen different stories. People love stories. People remember stories, case histories, examples, experiences—they forget generalities, explanations, philosophizing. Tell a story. Give an example. That's the secret of the interesting talk.

14. Tell a story on yourself once in a while. It wins the audience to you as a fellow human being. It takes the stuffiness out of heavy presentations. Don't tell only where you were right; tell where you were wrong.

15. Don't lean on things. Stand on your feet.

16. Make sure that your audience can see everything displayed.

17. Ask questions in your talk once in a while. And then give the answer in the form of a story.

18. Bring your audience into your talk, whenever you can. If they are men in your profession, there is much in common in past experiences remembered and present experiences faced that will provide a chance for a gracious and inclusive allusion.

19. If distractions occur, don't ignore them. Turn them into some timely or humorous aid. When a cat walked across the stage during a recital by Rubinoff, the violinist, he stopped playing, then swung into "Kitten on the Keys." He got a roar of laughter from his audience. Then they were ready to listen.

20. Look at your subject from the audience's viewpoint. What is there about it that will interest *them* specifically? Begin your talk with the angle that interests them most.

21. Don't try to cover too much. Select and illustrate with a wealth of anecdote and case history. The points should be few; the illustrations many and colorful.

22. Use figures sparingly. Try to convert them into some more dramatic method of illustration. Even though your audience may be able to read a balance sheet, don't make them do so.

23. Retain the colorful quirks and characteristics of your own personality, style of speaking, and use of language. A British accent or a southern drawl, if not unnatural or unintelligible, may be an asset. A regional choice of words or a unique touch of humor can often be extremely refreshing. Strip off your annoying mannerisms, but keep your personality color. Your audience wants your personality as much as they want your talk.

24. Be honest and unassuming. Avoid display for the sake of display or that appearance of slick professionalism that many inexperienced speakers feel necessary to the "putting over" of a speech. Be natural. It is you yourself that the audience came to hear—not some mythical professional spieler.

25. When you have reached the end, when the audience has responded to the full, cease.

THE MYSTERIOUS WORLD BELOW FORMAL CHANNELS

Choosing the level and form

Form is that golden vase wherein Thought,
that fleeting essence, is preserved to Posterity
ANATOLE FRANCE

The three levels of communicating . . .

"BEFORE EMPLOYING A WORD," JOSEPH Joubert remarked, "find a place for it."

Among the most baffling questions facing those who must reach others are: In what form and through what means can the individual or the group be reached? What channel or what medium does one use to get the message through? Experience seems to show it is not enough to have eloquence or skill in language; one must also know how to put these skills into the most effective channels. One must understand the levels and forms of communicating in the business, social, and organizational worlds and how to employ them.

It is often a source of wonder that certain men who do not express themselves well and are not eloquent can so frequently put over their messages so effectively in an organization. The answer generally lies in their knowledge of the forms and channels and of their use in that organization. The beautifully worded message sent in the form of a memorandum at a certain level of organization may have precisely the opposite effect intended or no effect at all because that message should have been transmitted only at the informal level and probably by word of mouth. A great idea may lie floating in the Sargasso Sea of informal communication, when it should have had a full-scale presentation before a board of directors. A substantial treatment which belongs in a book in the great world may be dissipated in a dozen little manuals or instruction guides because no one understood the potentialities of the main form.

Here the effectiveness of language, no matter how eloquent, and of substance, no matter how valuable, is destroyed by not understanding or suiting the proper form and medium to the content and not being aware of the proper channels through which people reach each other.

Let us, therefore, scout the terrain in our general business world and try to find our way through the various levels and forms which are basic to communicating and those which are in vogue today in our business society. They are the unorganized or informal level of communicating, the organized level of communicating with its seven basic forms, and the level at which opinion or taste leaders are usually reached, where art and style are important.

THE MYSTERIOUS WORLD OF UNORGANIZED COMMUNICATING

The first, and by far the most common, level of communicating is that which goes on below the conscious control of social mechanisms and channels. Perhaps 70 per cent of the communication in an organization occurs at this informal, unorganized level. The formal, organized communication, together with that level at which art and style are important, represents the frosting on the cake.

It is well recognized that wherever men are gathered together and whether there are organized forms and recognized channels available or not, communicating goes on all the time. In fact, at the unorganized level of communicating, a large but unrecognized portion of all the work as well as all the action of the organization is carried out. Consider the following:

"Bill, how about scrounging up some extra parts for Number 4 shop for tomorrow. I know it's not according to the book, but we'll do your group a favor when the Benson order comes in." Result: a shop meets its quota on time.

"It's a great organization. I worked there a couple of years ago. They have some pretty hot ideas cooking in their labs. You can't go wrong with them." Result: a promising engineer leaves his present job to go with a young company.

"Well, I'll tell you, Jim, he was with me for awhile, but I just . . . well I don't know. I wouldn't want to queer his chances." Result: the man about whom they are speaking does not get the promotion.

"My feeling is we're stuck in the mud. We need new goals, new directions. We're just not with it. The Old Man may have been great ten years ago, but damn it he's getting old." Result: a friend on the board persuades the president to set a date for retirement.

These examples suggest the kind of significant action triggered at this level. They only suggest it, for the variety and depth of the action stimulated at the informal level can be immense, and varies according to the formal channels available. Thus, it is obvious that the man of affairs cannot become truly effective unless he learns to operate here.

Let us look more closely, therefore, at this level, for there are categories of idea and thought, information and instruction which might well be unacceptable if communicated at any other level. It may be said that England was ruled for generations from the country houses of the great gentry and peers and that much of its policy and action came from a word dropped here and there between gentlemen. The counterparts of these situations are not unknown in modern organizations today.

It might well be a mistake, for example, to send through channels a formal memorandum concerning an expensive blunder if you wished to retain the services of the man who made it. An informal discussion might be more fruitful.

It might well be disastrous to send out to an important recipient a report concerning a course of action he is known to oppose violently without first having warned him through informal means of communication that you are making this move.

How, then, can the man of affairs learn the ropes in the world below the company's dialogue structure? How can he keep contact with that flow of conversation below the hierarchy channels? Here are three main procedures which can give him that necessary grasp of what is going on and the opportunities and the ability to operate here:

1. He must circulate freely in the organization; this is often termed "getting out into the field."

2. He must speak the languages of the various groups. When he enters the laboratories, for instance, it would help if he could talk the language of the research men. A leader during his rise in the field in which he has his career learns to absorb the language and vocabulary of the world through which he moves, and he does this through each field and in each area to which his progress takes him.

3. He must keep up with what is going on in the great world outside. He must read, read, read; talk to people in related fields; attend important outside meetings and gatherings; be alert to what is new in the world of science, art, and ideas, and especially to how his own profession will be influenced by these new winds of change.

Let us examine more closely these three ways of remaining effective at the unformalized level of communication.

Getting into the field

The amount of information a man of affairs can secure at the level below the organized forms and channels of communication depends to a large degree on the number, variety, and nature of his contacts. As a man rises in his career, his administrative demands tend to seal him off from vital information which either cannot be carried through formal channels or are overlooked by them. Here are some examples of the kind of information which has been discovered by going into the field:

The president of a growing company on an impulse decided to stop over at one of the smaller laboratories on his way back from a trip to his largest plant. At the laboratories, he fell into conversation with a young lab assistant who remarked casually that it was too bad they were not in the paper business, as one of their new processes would lend itself to a special item there. Result: an entire new product for the company, one which eventually became one of its most profitable.

The financial vice president of a large company had lunch with a friend in a related business downtown. "Why don't you go into the money field like us?" he said. "Here's what we did." Result: for the company, a cutting down of the unprofitable "float" of cash between payrolls and investment of funds that brought better money management and some profit.

The president of a huge corporation stopped off to look at a building being demolished on the company property. "It'd be cheaper to burn it down," the well-dressed stranger next to him said jokingly. "If it's anything like our warehouse, the insurance has been worth more than the building for ten years." Result: an investigation of the insurance carried by this big company revealing half a hundred locations which were either overinsured or inappropriately insured and savings of millions by more careful use of insurance.

The administrative vice president was watching some painters painting cable reels in the powerhouse yard. "Nice color you have there," he said jocularly to the foreman. "How often d'you paint them?" "Every year sure as shootin'," the foreman answered. "Don't know why though. These reels are obsolete. Ought to throw 'em out." Result: reels were sold and a few thousand dollars in painting and inventory costs saved.

The chairman of the board turned to the young man in the cafeteria and said: "Pardon me, but I couldn't help overhearing your comment. Why wouldn't this friend of yours you speak so highly of come with us?" The young man looked at the distinguished older man for a moment. "Well sir," he said, "my friend's an idea man, and they keep saying they like ideas around here, but they really don't and everybody knows it." Result: a new manager for that division and a thorough shakeup throughout the company.

Most of the information gathered in this informal fashion by executives and men of affairs would not ordinarily have come to them through organized channels of communication. What is well known out in the field and what is current around the industry may never reach headquarters. The use of the unorganized form of communicating requires, in part, getting out in the field at regular intervals.

Speaking the language

It also requires being multilingual in the world of affairs, speaking both the language of the trade or business and also the language of the men at various levels of background. This does not, of course, mean using bad grammar or an uneducated accent or any usage beneath the dignity of the highest cultivation a person possesses. It means having a knowledge of and an interest in the areas of activity and the worlds which concern the administrator and into which he must move from time to time.

In the oil industry, for example, the man of affairs will know not only the principles and business concepts involved but also the colorful language and the tone and atmosphere of the industry. Of course, he will know what a farmout is, but he will also know what finishing barefooted means. Of course he will know how to handle leasehold and concession costs, but he will also know what they are referring to when they say whiskey stick.

In the television industry, the administrator may know the accounting problems, but he will also know the style and concepts and way of life in the field and the colorful or apt expressions in which they are illuminated. He may know about the treatment of theatrical film costs, but he will also know what the crawl is or what is meant by full screen ID, the answer print, or the phrase "across the board," and he will be able to use these expressions in his ordinary conversation.

This may seem elementary, but it is surprising how fast the feel of the language dims and the colors fade and one is no longer able to enter that world and understand its voices. The languages of our professions, trades, and fields are multiplying as our economic and scientific worlds grow more complex and sophisticated, but every man of affairs must keep fresh his grasp and understanding of the languages in his areas of concern if he is to operate effectively at the level of informal communicating.

Keeping open contacts to the great world

Finally, to operate in the world beyond the organization's dialogue structure, the man of affairs must keep abreast of what is going on in the Great World, the world of opinion leaders and taste leaders. We shall deal in more detail with the importance of tapping this source of information, knowledge, and thinking when we discuss communicating at the level where art and style are important. Suffice it to say here that a man cannot operate effectively in the area beyond organized communications channels and mechanisms unless he is attuned to the vital ideas and thoughts, the changes and fashions of the important worlds outside his own.

John Maynard Keynes' famous remark on the power of ideas has added relevance in this area when we realize how deeply we and our affairs are influenced not only by thinkers long gone, but by those coming up. "Practical men," Keynes said, "who believe themselves to be quite exempt from any intellectual influences, are usually the slaves of some defunct economist." And extending that thought, it is important for the man of affairs to keep open his channels to the flow of new thought and discovery in the Great World, for he and his industry may be deeply influenced or changed by the ideas which have their origin far outside his immediate interests. All of us in our closed-in worlds dance to tunes that were played by greater minds and talents than our own from far outside our particular spheres, and all of us are influenced also even by lesser leaders in less-related or less-important fields. The thinking in government and in education, to mention just two vital areas, is important to the concerns of any man of affairs.

So, at the level of unorganized communicating, the administrator must keep abreast of fields outside his own; read widely and extensively; attend conventions, gatherings, and cultural seminars; and give attention to this crucial aspect of his development. These particular contacts become vital to his ability to communicate at the level required to influence those who can be of great benefit to him and his affairs.

USING THE FORMS AND CHANNELS OF ORGANIZED COMMUNICATIONS

The fact that perhaps 70 per cent of all communicating in an organization is at the unformalized level below or beyond the structured communications channels and mechanisms should not blind the man of affairs or the organization to the importance of organized forms and channels or to that body of communication in which art and style are important. These areas of communicating may be the frosting on the cake, but they are so vital in an organization of any size or substance and to a man who hopes to reach any important segments of those who contribute to an enterprise or to the world's thinking that without them most serious ventures would be all but unfeasible.

There will, of course, be communication going on all the time, whether or not there are forms or recognized channels available, but without the forms and channels, there can be little control. In fact, if these forms or channels are insufficient or irrational, a heavy communications overload at the informal level will result, a communications overload that may lead to a breakdown in effectiveness where there is no way of separating rumor from fact, setting up priorities of importance of operations or data, distinguishing between the trivial and the vital, etc. In extreme cases, it may lead to complete chaos and disintegration.

Most large and complex organizations have had to develop, as a matter of survival, these forms and channels, but it is surprising how many organizations of medium size or organizations which are growing rapidly have failed to develop this area of their organizational life. For without sufficient communications forms and channels, the organization cannot secure quickly enough or use the information necessary to keep the enterprise going. Communication is the glue which holds the structure together, and a good sound communications system is absolutely vital to any collective operation.

The seven basic forms today

We shall deal with the common organization channels of communication later, but here we would do well to enumerate the seven common business forms of communication which the business leader must employ today to reach the various groups important to him. They are the *conference, business correspondence,* the *memorandum and report,* the *promotional piece,* the *article,* the *speech,* before various audiences, and, for large and important ideas or information, the *book.* We shall deal briefly with each in succeeding chapters of this part after we have considered the third level of communicating, the level at which art and style are important.

THE LEVEL WHERE ART AND STYLE ARE IMPORTANT

We now approach the third level of communicating to which the man of affairs should address himself throughout his career. This is the level at which opinion and taste leaders can be reached, the level where art and style are important. What, we may ask ourselves, distinguishes this world from the two others we have been talking about—the great jungle of unformalized communicating and the more ordered world of organized communicating with its seven basic forms? The answer is simple: quality. This third level requires distinction of mind, character, and style, and the problem posed goes beyond technique. How then can this elevated world be reached? What elements and characteristics can be discriminated? How can style be developed?

We cannot marshal here, unfortunately, any cut-and-dried rules, but there are informal approaches which, experience seems to show, develop the characteristics leading to this level. Let us look at them.

The problem of style

In all professions and walks of life during all ages, men of cultivation have taken a pride in their style of writing and have devoted disinterested time and attention to it. They have considered it an important part of their equipment as cultivated men. They have spent—even the busiest and most widely sought of them—some time in the development of a style that is an ornament and a fitting medium for the display of their abilities. They have developed this style in the same way that all cultivated men of all ages have developed their style—through practice. They did not write only when they had to. They wrote—perhaps in their journals at quiet moments or in the service of some disinterested study they were making for themselves alone—carefully and sometimes laboriously at regular periods and over the whole span of their active lives.

It is not enough to say that the pace of modern life makes this impossible, because today, perhaps more generally than ever, since education has become the province of the many, the top men in all fields are doing the same. In the professions of law and medicine, the literary and professional efforts of jurists, attorneys, and doctors ornament briefs and dissertations, become articles and reports in the scholarly and popular journals, and appear in book form, often even on the best seller lists. They challenge literary men in their own fields. This seems to be less true in business, and there is no reason that it should be. The development of an analytical mind and the ability to handle "the language of business" are not inimical to good writing, though the objective analytical man must beware of allowing his critical abilities to freeze his creative powers.

The question of time

The problem seems to be that those in business feel they have no time for this basic pursuit and cannot see, until it is too late, what use it will be to them in their careers or in the world. First, they have no time to read. And by that we mean reading not simply in business, professional, or technical journals or texts but in the fields of popular and classical literature, so that some of the thought and language patterns of skilled and substantial writers rub off on them. No one can become a good writer without being a great reader. A man who does not read in the fields of contemporary literature simply cannot acquire those overtones of rhythm and thought that give flavor and effectiveness to a style. It is not necessary or especially desirable to "study" such works; it is more important to build the reading habit and to enjoy the books read. Whether a man reads Tolstoy, Nabokov, Pearl Buck, Thomas Mann, or the latest popular novel is not so important as that he read in quantity and enjoy what he reads. But the cry always is: "When do I have time?" And the answer always must be: "You have to make the time. It won't be given you." A man of affairs simply cannot afford not to read.

The second horn of the dilemma is that the man coming up puts aside no time to write. And by writing we refer to the unassigned sort of writing done, say, of a Sunday evening in journals or the writing that consists of trying one's hand at an essay or study or article for the sake of the subject and the self-expression alone. Of course, it may turn out to amount to something. The chances are greater it will not. But the long-suffering wife who has to listen to it or perhaps the sympathetic associate who says: "Very nice—yes, very nice indeed," is doing something very valuable. She or he is listening to a mind and a skill that are developing. And the man himself is building a reservoir of skill and thought that will mark him out from his colleagues two ... three ... five years later. When someone asks him to: "Put together something for me on this . . .," this man's work will be distinguished by years of practice.

Hazards of criticism

At this point, the man coming up, who throws himself seriously into an effort to increase his writing skills, will face one of the great hazards of the neophyte—unskilled and sometimes brutal criticism.

Obviously, a man's early efforts to produce usable or even readable writing will in all probability be appalling. They will not only offend his own sensibilities and arouse his own critical faculties against himself but will also tend to arouse the scorn and sometimes the ridicule of his superiors. We have already warned against the dangers of overuse of one's own critical faculties. These faculties, it has been pointed out, should not be aroused too early or they will kill the creative flow, and they must not be allowed to set up emotional and psychological reactions which may kill the desire to try again and even make all writing distasteful. The so-called perfectionist often slaughters that poor goose whose golden eggs are the desire, energy, and willingness to try again. High standards may be important, but they are not to be used to bludgeon a man at the beginning of the long hard road to the third level of communicating.

The second aspect of this hazard—the unskilled criticism and ridicule of one's work by others—is equally dangerous, and the rising man must become thick-skinned enough to sustain such criticism without letting it dampen his determination or the pleasure he will soon find in the exercise of his writing skills. Most of those who have become good writers have at some time, in the common expression, "learned the hard way" by having their work torn up before their eyes or having some temperamental superior scream with anguish and drop their effort neatly into the wastebasket. This sort of response, of course, is the most effective possible way to dry up creative effort.

A man is more sensitive about his writing than about almost any other ability or skill he may have. He may be insulted about his business competence, but he cannot without its seriously affecting him be insulted about his writing. And a good man, usually being more sensitive, may be far more crushed by having his written work bludgeoned than one who has no pride. Pride of authorship, far from being something that must be beaten out of the rising man, is a quality that should be encouraged. If a man has no pride in what he writes, his writing is not apt to be very good.

But the effect is even more serious than that, and some survive it, while others do not. If a man works hard and produces a piece which when presented to the reviewer is treated either with contempt or with distaste, the next time he is asked to produce something, he will freeze up. And if his work is continually—and sometimes unnecessarily—changed, he will reach the stage very quickly where he hates writing and avoids it whenever he can. He may quit and get into a part of the business world where writing demands are not so great. Or, having been frozen in an area so essential to his development as a person, he may stop growing.

Thus, in the early climb up the long road to art and style, it is important to develop the self-confidence and iron nerves of the man who is bound to succeed in any effort he undertakes. A man who is to reach the third level must possess not only talent but also drive, determination, and unshakable self-confidence. Like any superior achievement, art and style are the product of talent, luck, and what can only be described in the vernacular: guts.

An informal, lifelong program

Obviously, then, it is of great importance for the man of affairs to begin early learning to express himself through written language, and we offer here a basic informal program for establishing a good foundation. This program must be a permanent one. At the risk of being considered wildly visionary, we might suggest that the businessman develop four vital habits:

1. The *reading* of books in popular or classical literature at the rate of one every two weeks (twenty-five books per year). These books may be paperbacks, popular novels, history, etc., but must *not* be technical or merely professional reading. Such reading is designed to give the businessman "the reading habit" and an enjoyment of books. He quickly acquires familiarity with the thought and language patterns of the day. It is not necessary to set aside prescribed time to read. One very useful device for building the habit is always to have a book with you and to dip into it from time to time during the day while you are waiting for a friend or during trips or between appointments. The ability to dip into a work and im-

mediately lose oneself in it opens up a great vista of different worlds, and those who have this habit may absorb two or three books a week without even realizing it.

2. The *writing* in journals or on some disinterested project for an hour each Sunday evening.

3. The *studying* of the varied and numerous books on writing and the keeping of a "line journal" to copy out unusual and vivid thoughts and expressions.

4. The *consulting* with more experienced associates for comment and assistance on specific writing and speaking assignments.

This program, even when pursued over the years, only supplies a foundation for the climb to the third plane of communicating. You begin to compose a symphony by practicing the scales. What is required is that all through a man's career he pay attention to these pursuits, that he speak often and produce a substantial body of written work, that he keep a window open on the Great World and remain aware of the tides of thought and action of his times. Again, distinguished writing or communicating is the product of distinguished minds and distinguished abilities and is not given to us all, even the most deserving and hard-working. But it has certain characteristics in the actual use of language which are well worth cultivating. It is usually simple and basic. It usually drives to the heart of important meanings. It has color, candor, and sweep.

George Orwell, the noted British author, in a review converted a famous passage of the Bible into the kind of ordinary decent business jargon which we use. Here it is, as Orwell rendered it:

Objective consideration of contemporary phenomena compels the conclusion that success or failure in competitive activities exhibits no tendency to be commensurate with innate capacity, but that a considerable element of the unpredictable must inevitably be taken into account.

There is nothing especially wrong with this. A little heavy

perhaps. It speaks to us in the generalities we so dearly love. It uses our rather ponderous wording. It lacks color. But here is how Ecclesiastes said it—the difference between ordinary writing and great writing:

> I returned and saw under the sun that the race is not to the swift nor the battle to the strong, neither yet bread to the wise nor yet riches to men of understanding nor yet favor to men of skill but time and chance happeneth to them all.

It is at this level—at this third level—that the whole man is reached.

FOUR KEY QUESTIONS ABOUT ANY COMMUNICATION

Finally, and before taking up the first of the seven basic forms of business communication, it may be well to consider these questions which should be asked about any communication:

To whom am I speaking? This requires more analysis than may appear on the surface, since you are often addressing not only the direct recipient of the message but sometimes others who will eventually see or have to act upon it or be guided by it.

What is the value of this communication? "Value" is the operative word here. What will the message actually do for the recipient? This is more fundamental even than stating the purpose of the message, since the *value* may be different from the purpose, and the purpose is less relevant than the value to the one who receives it.

What is the point or conclusion? This question, of course, requires that you give the reader in one or two sentences the substance of the whole communication, "what it is all about."

Finally, can the substance of the whole communication be immediately grasped by the reader through skimming the title or heads and subheads? A communication which gives little or no immediate clue to its substance is generally read with difficulty and reluctance.

Asking and answering these questions will give the business leader a quick start in selecting and organizing material for use in the various forms. Now to the seven forms.

5

"A group of the unfit, appointed by the unwilling to do the unnecessary" . . .

"MINDS THAT HAVE NOTHING TO CONFER," Wordsworth wrote, "have little to perceive," and though the poet was speaking poetically, his thought applies to many who attend and chair conferences.

The conference has been the butt of a great variety of exasperated and only half jocular humor. It has been called "a meeting to decide when the next meeting will be held," "a meeting of a group of men who singly can do nothing but who collectively agree that nothing can be done," "a device to substitute the pleasures of companionship for the loneliness of toil and the dreariness of thought," and lately "a group of the unfit, appointed by the unwilling, to do the unnecessary," and unfortunately in all too many instances the humor cuts too close to the truth.

From the viewpoint of the man of affairs as an administrator, however, the conference is probably one of the most frequently employed and effective of the seven common forms of communication. Whether it is a full board of directors meeting in all its stately splendor or a section group's quick, weekly get-together, whether it is the gathering of the president's "cabinet" or a "brainstorming" session of the creative people, whether it is the monthly department heads' meeting or the group discussion session to iron out an emergency, the conference—and it takes innumerable forms—remains one of the basic, if not the basic, communications tool in modern business. Thus, the man of affairs would do well to have some knowledge of how to call, prepare for, and run a conference and know and understand its basic usefulness.

Conferences may be considered of three sorts, depending on their purposes: the formal recurring organization conference for the purpose of overseeing a business or directing an organization, such as a cabinet meeting or a board of directors meeting; second, the irregular group or committee meeting to deal with problems on an advisory basis; and, third, the group discussion or convention for the purpose of securing knowledge and exchanging thoughts and experience. It is important to distinguish among the three kinds, since the methods of preparation, direction, and results of each have basic differences.

The conference as a form as considered here implies participation, although there are meetings called conferences which are simply gatherings of a number of persons to receive instructions or orders from higher authority, on the one hand, and those, on the other, which are actually lectures, where nothing is demanded of those present except the ability to hear. Such gatherings do not lie within the form we discuss in this chapter. They are not working tools, and the conference, as dealt with here, is distinctly a working communications form.

*W*HAT YOU SHOULD KNOW ABOUT THE FORMAL CONFERENCE

The first type we shall deal with is the formal, generally recurring administrative conference. It is usually of major importance in the life of an organization and is extremely demanding of its participants. Taking the board of directors or board of governors meeting as typical, let us look carefully at the characteristics, demands, and values of this sort of conference.

Administrative conferences generally should not have more than twenty members, and the range should perhaps be from eight to twenty, although certain large corporations, in order to secure the widest possible variety of experience, have had as many as twenty-eight members on the board. Boards of directors of corporations exemplify in many ways the demands of this kind of conference in a truly concentrated form, and before going into an effective use of this type of administrative communications form, let us briefly look at such a board's duties. Legally, the board is charged with the overall management and direction of the company, under a specific charter and bylaws. As such, each director is required to act with due care and undivided loyalty in the interests of the corporation and must give the corporation's business the same energy, diligence, enterprise, and carefulness he would, as a prudent person, give his own affairs.

One of the characteristics of such conferences is that they vary in the participation of each member. While such a board is invested with the highest authority, under a strong or autocratic chairman (particularly if he is also the chief executive officer of the company), the board may become merely a rubber stamp for operating management. On the other hand, the board may so dominate the executive officers that it hampers them in that direction of the company to which the board itself has assigned them.

Where such extremes occur, the conference as an instrument, of course, breaks down. Like all conferences, this administrative meeting should have a carefully researched and prepared agenda. Often, forms are devised for presenting all material to board members so that their substance can be quickly grasped and the action which they are being requested to take or the problem they are being asked to solve may be highlighted. Even background materials as well as pertinent information are presented in this format.

In these meetings, the degree of formality may vary, but in general they are more successful when run with moderate formality during voting procedure and with informality at discussion and briefing periods. The administrative conference tends to break down when the agenda is not sufficiently and carefully prepared, when factions form or dissension arises beyond the confines of the board's purposes, or when struggles for power destroy the morale of the group as a whole. Five suggestions can be made for securing such a conference's effectiveness:

1. Hold this type of conference on a regularly scheduled basis, so members can plan to meet their obligations to attend.

2. See that each member is familiar with the qualifications and attainments of his fellow members.

3. See that all matters coming before the board are fully and carefully researched and presented.

4. See that sufficient discussion takes place to insure a thorough airing of the board's view on each matter presented.

5. See that the results as expressed either in the minutes of the meeting or (where minutes are not required) in summary reports are clearly presented and reach each member.

Members of this type of conference must communicate with each other, and a consensus must be reached which will bring decisions on such vital moves as mergers, capital expenditures, reorganization of a company, and the like.

The smaller or less-exalted counterparts of this type of administrative conference are numerous and at all levels. Section supervisors, heads of departments, plant managers, and heads of divisions all may use this type of conference to make and communicate policy and procedure for their areas of responsibility. Skill in participating or handling such conferences arises chiefly from experience, but some of the techniques will be discussed in more detail in the studies of the next two types of conferences.

*W*HAT YOU SHOULD KNOW ABOUT ADVISORY CONFERENCES

Perhaps most typical of the advisory kind of conference are the meetings of the thousands of voluntary civic committees which in the United States play such a crucial role in local, state, and even national affairs. These committees may range from the local library board, board of education, or committee to bring business to our town to the governor's advisory committee on juvenile delinquency, slum clearance, or taxation to a national conference on international cooperation. In the United States, a great deal of the work of the community is done by these voluntary committee conferences, and no man of affairs who wishes to play a part in the world can have escaped serving on one or another of them.

To indicate what skills and techniques are called on to operate effectively in such conferences, let us look at a representative advisory conference which has been called to develop some means for bringing business back to a dying town that has just lost its largest industrial establishment, a corduroy mill. The conference has been called by the mayor, and present are the town newspaper publisher and editor; the managers of the branches of the two chain stores in town; a town attorney; a local public accountant; the proprietors of the corner stationery store, the drugstore, and the hardware store; and the president of the local bank.

The mayor opens the meeting thus:

> Gentlemen, this meeting has been called, as you know, to see what can be done, what measures can be taken somehow to make up for the loss of the Greenville Mill. We did our best to keep it here, but now recriminations and hand-wringing are not going to get us anywhere. What's done is done. There are 800 people out of jobs. Emergency measures have all been taken. Those who can be placed immediately have been placed. Many have left to go to the new plant down South. The company has given us all the help it was able to. Our problem, it seems to me, is no longer what short-term, immediate steps we can take to remedy one situation but what immediate steps we can take to plan a long-term program to attract new business to this town, and as leading citizens I have asked you to serve on a committee to undertake and help put into effect such a program.... You have before you an agenda which suggests a framework for our discussions, and you have all received, following your acceptance of service on this committee, a fairly heavy packet of background material, which I hope you have been able to look at....

So the meeting opens. Let us now go back and see something of what lies behind such a conference. First of all, the men selected were chosen because they had a history of service to the town and were effective and willing. The conference as a form of communication must be made up of the right persons. Men who will not do the work, who are there simply as figureheads often destroy the morale of the group and negate the effectiveness of this form. It is well known, of course, that quite often a "leading citizen" or a "gray eminence" who will not or cannot really contribute to the work must sometimes be added to such a group either because his prestige lends a certain public relations value in the effort or because, if he were not placed upon the committee, he might actively oppose the work. However, in general, it is best to form a committee for such conferences only of workers.

Second, such a conference to be effective must be carefully prepared for. In this case, the mayor had researched and collected the following kinds of information to be sent to the prospective conference members: (1) background material on three specific proposals to bring business to the town, (2) two studies on the kinds of businesses suitable for towns of that size and area, (3) three case studies of how towns launched new business and business revival programs successfully, (4) a list of agencies, national, state, and private, which offer assistance to communities in planning, rehabilitation, etc. In addition, the mayor had included a number of suggestions made by members of the council and others on the subject and copies of letters from citizens with suggestions about the village, which had come in over the years.

Third, in the handling of the invitations, the place of meeting, and later the place of the conference itself, the mayor did everything in his power to set a tone which indicated that this committee was to be accorded the highest prestige and that its conclusions and proposals would enjoy the widest publicity and the greatest consideration. These may be said to be the three indispensable approaches necessary to use this form effectively in this class of conference.

Mr. George Gallup quoted the former Lieutenant Governor of New York, the Honorable Frank C. Moore, President of the Government Affairs Foundation, on the following do's and don'ts of handling committees and conferences:

1. Don't ask any advisory committee of citizens to deal with an easy problem. These committees are more suc-

cessful when they concern themselves with difficult ones, especially those that official agencies have been unable to solve.

2. Don't coax anyone to serve, or accept anyone as a member of the committee unless he agrees to attend every meeting and to give his full effort.

3. Avoid choosing persons who stand to profit personally from the committee's action, or who have to clear their votes with any organization they may represent.

4. It is not necessary to select persons who are expert or even especially well-informed about the problem under study, provided that they are intelligent, objective, and favorably known to a substantial segment of the persons concerned with the problem.

5. The number of members to include can vary, but experience in New York State would indicate that fifteen is a workable and effective number.

6. Committee meetings should be held at a place that is not too comfortable or attractive, and they should be free of the diversions usually offered by palatial country clubs and summer resorts.

7. At the first two or three committee meetings, basic, factual information should be presented through a series of carefully prepared memoranda, which are later supplied to all members. To make certain that every member is familiar with the content, the memoranda should be read aloud to the entire committee.

8. The first meetings should be designed solely to clarify the understanding of committee members. In this process, as Governor Moore states, "It has always been amazing to see how problems diminish in size and complexity as the actual facts are disclosed and understood."

9. After the presentation of the facts has been completed (which may require several meetings), the discussion should begin—but not before this time. At the conclusion of each of the later meetings the chairman should

review and "peg down" the points upon which agreement has been reached, keeping for later discussion the points of disagreement.

10. From the beginning to the end of the committee's task, the chairman should not forget that the goal is the solution of the problem and not the writing of a report "to be abandoned, like a foundling child, on the doorstep of some other agency."

11. The report should be designed with the thought in mind to broaden the knowledge and understanding of the problem on the part of public officials and citizens and "to encourage and equip the authorized agencies to take effective action upon the recommendation of the committee."

12. The report that emerges should be as attractive and as readable as it can be made. It should be written in clear, concise language with avoidance of "officialese." It should be distributed widely. The salient points in the report itself can be supplied to the newspaper and other media of communication as soon as the committee has reached agreement on the findings.

*W*HAT YOU SHOULD KNOW ABOUT GROUP DISCUSSION CONFERENCES

The third sort of conference is the information seminar, the basic purpose of which is to develop information and knowledge, and to exchange experience on a subject. Such conferences range from graduate class discussions through company department information meetings to professional development discussion groups. Their care and handling also provide valuable lessons in the care and handling of all kinds of conferences.

A manual on *How To Be A Good Group Discussion Leader* opens as follows:

The object of a good group discussion session is, first, to elicit and transmit information on important matters within our field and, secondly, to give members of the group experience and technique in expressing themselves and in handling themselves under conference conditions. [Our] purpose is to give the man responsible for conducting these meetings ... tips on [their] organization and direction. ... Our hints may be gathered under three headings: first, how to prepare for the group, conclude and summarize a group discussion. ...

The following suggestions are made on the subject of preparation:

> Preparation includes: (1) researching the material (2) preparing agenda for those who will attend (3) assigning reading material to prospective members of the group (4) assigning specific research and stimulus questions to key members of the group and (5) seeing that the facilities of the meeting room are adequate for the group's requirements.

In the matter of handling the conference, the man of affairs must develop certain techniques in launching the meeting, maintaining the pace and flow, and finally eliciting the substantial material the members of the group have to offer.

In general, opening remarks should be brief and to the point. The purpose and what it is hoped will be accomplished must be spelled out effectively. The area of discussion should be clearly indicated. Then the moderator must open the conference for discussion. He may do so by going around the table and asking comments on the initial aspect of the subject. Or he may throw the subject open for voluntary response. Once he has done this, the second area of his responsibility has been reached: he must maintain the pace and flow of the discussion.

There have been a great many suggestions on how to maintain this pace and flow and how to keep control of a group discussion conference sufficiently to enable the members to get the most from it. Suffice it to say here that the man of affairs must make sure he himself prepares for, understands, and contributes fully to any conference in which he plays a part. The conference is and can be one of the most powerful and effective communication tools at the business leader's command. Unfortunately, in many cases, for want of preparation, for lack of rudimentary skills or experience, too many in business have misused this form, wasting by ineptness, lack of preparation, lack of consideration, and lack of care one of the world's most valuable commodities—the time of its useful, important, and busy men.

6

"A multitude of barbarous and dark words" . . .

"THE NEED OF COMPOSING LETTERS," MECROS said, "was the earliest and most constant incentive to terseness, clarity and exactitude of statement." And Francis Bacon wrote: "Letters such as written by wise men are, of all the words of men, in my judgment the best."

It is true that the letter has been one of the most effective forms of communication throughout the centuries of men's affairs, whether it is George Washington writing from Valley Forge to his critics in Congress or Leonardo da Vinci asking the Duke of Milan for a job.

> We find gentlemen [Washington wrote] without knowing whether the army was really going into winter quarters or not reprobating the measure as if they thought soldiers were made of stocks or stones. . . . I can assure these gentlemen that it is a much easier and less distressing thing to draw remonstrances in a comfortable room by a good fireside than to occupy a cold bleak hill and sleep under frost and snow without clothes or blankets. . . .

And Leonardo da Vinci indicated to the Duke of Milan some of his accomplishments and qualifications as follows:

> Having, most illustrious lord, seen and considered the experiments of those who pose as masters in the art of inventing instruments of war, and finding that their inventions differ in no way from those in common use, I am emboldened . . . to solicit an appointment of acquainting your Excellency with certain of my secrets. . . .

1. I can construct bridges which are light and strong
   . . .
2. In case of siege I can cut off water from the trenches
   and make pontoons and scaling ladders . . .
3. I can demolish every fortress if its foundations have
   not been set in stone. . . .

and so on for seven more "inventions" with a final offer to demonstrate them.

Such letters played crucial parts in the tides of men's affairs, and it is true that today the letter still plays a role in men's affairs, and there are still men who can write letters with style and flair. However, as the ordinary form for short messages in business, the role of the letter has changed somewhat, and other instruments, because of the enormous increase in the requirements of volume and speed in correspondence, have come to share with the business letter its business role. Such instruments are, of course, the telephone, which now bears the largest volume of short message communication, the TWX, the telegram and cable. The letter, nevertheless, still holds a crucial place as a form of business communication, and the man of affairs has the problem now not only of being able to prepare and compose letters, but even more important of managing correspondence, which is a somewhat broader operation. Let us first look at this operation and then turn back to the letter as the crowning form in this method of communicating.

*H*OW TO MANAGE VOLUME CORRESPONDENCE

The dilemma of management correspondence today may be viewed from two aspects: that of the organization and that of the man of affairs.

In the case of one bank with 3,000 employees, some 2.5 million letters a year go out. If a conservative estimate of the cost is put at $1.25 per letter (employee's time, postage, paper, etc.), then the bank spends more than $3 million a year on letters. This, of course, is a very conservative guess, but the point is that letter writing in business may or may not be economically sound, depending on how the correspondence is managed.

Correspondence issuing from an organization should have several key characteristics: a suitable tone and quality, clarity, timeliness, effectiveness, and low cost. These are not easy to come by if the issuing of correspondence is unorganized, uncoordinated, and unchecked, and those who administer an organization would do well to consider the following possible steps to control the quality and cost of this important form.

1. Have produced courteous and effective printed forms for repetitive correspondence, such as requests for printed material, acknowledgement of inquiries, and the like.

2. Develop suitable replies for often-asked questions or often-solicited advice where this is part of the organization's routine business.

3. Develop standard formats for certain kinds of common correspondence to enable inexperienced writers to handle it easily and effectively.

4. Develop model letters for all important communications for use by those responsible in key areas. These letters might serve only as guides, but they would embody the best and most effective tone, quality of content, organization, and writing that the talent of the organization can provide and act as a standard for the less experienced.

5. Prepare a correspondence guide with a few hints and suggestions on keeping down the wordage and the volume of correspondence to reasonable and effective levels.

6. Set up a system for exchange of carbons or copies of important letters among key executives to keep them informed of current matters.

The common difficulty from the organization viewpoint is overcommunicating as well as communicating badly in this form. A guide on correspondence, as suggested for those members most responsible for the issuance of such correspondence, is often most helpful and welcome. The attention of a top executive or one especially talented in this form would save the organization substantial costs in this area and raise the tone and quality of its short message communications.

*H*OW TO HANDLE YOUR PERSONAL CORRESPONDENCE

The problem which faces the business leader today in handling correspondence requires some attention to planning and organization on his part also. He receives a good volume of communications week in and week out requiring acknowledgement or response. If he were as prolific as George Bernard Shaw and as witty (Shaw was reputed to have written more than 10,000 letters in his lifetime), he might be able to manage this volume by mail and do it with style and effect, although if he is to do everything else of importance, he probably cannot.

We have mentioned earlier that the letter should share the characteristics of all good writing. It should have the proper tone; it should have completeness, conciseness, concreteness, and readability, and we have indicated roughly what these are. One of the principal characteristics of the modern business letter is the increased warmth of tone and informality of the genre as a whole. Tone is important in any communication, and it is particularly important in a letter. To illustrate inappropriateness of tone, one professional man "discovered" this *Love Letter of an Accountant:*

Dear Mary:

As stated in my previous letter dated March 3rd, 19X2, I should greatly appreciate your consideration of certain matters discussed by us on the last occasion of our mutual propinquity.

You may remember that we agreed that our previous conferences had led us to believe that there is a substantial basis for a continued and perhaps fruitful series of meetings in which fundamental cooperation might, eventually, on a long-term consideration, result in a possible future legal status.

Nothing has come to my attention which precludes such possibility and I therefore look forward to hearing from you at an early opportunity, remaining

> Very truly yours,
> John

copies to respondent's parents

No answer to this letter, it seems, has been found.

However, today there appears little likelihood that the old formality will continue to bog down and depress recipients of business letters. The telephone has increased acquaintanceship and the personal tone, and modern letters are on the whole much more informal and warmer in address.

What is meant, however, by completeness and conciseness in a letter? They would seem to be obvious. Yet too many correspondents leave out essential information, and too many still run on for three pages where one would do. The man of affairs has read many a letter in which a date has been left out or a piece of essential knowledge assumed. Here is a request that the recipient look over an enclosed proposal and give his thoughts, but the letter contains no hint of how soon those thoughts are needed. Again, a letter explaining an ingenious financial procedure, but in it no hint of the value of this procedure to the organization. Such examples can unfortunately be multiplied.

On the other hand, the administrator has also read many a letter where the writer obviously did not have the time to organize the content properly or work out what he wanted to say, thus making the letter short and to the point. So the reader must wade through three pages of extraneous information to see what it was all about. Such letter writing is inexcusable today. Like the man who holds his business associate on the telephone forever, the disorganized letter writer is an exhausting and often agonizing nuisance, and it is the part of a gentleman to be sure we ourselves do not commit these misdemeanors. A letter can be short and still have wit and style and say all it has to say. If it cannot, perhaps it would be better to discuss the matter over the telephone or consider a meeting.

Finally, on the subject of concreteness in a letter, it is

often of inestimable value to give a brief example or to illustrate what one is talking about. A new zoning plan is urged. How the zoning plan worked in a nearby neighborhood could make all the difference in illustrating its worth. Concreteness—the giving of examples and illustrations—illuminates letters as it does every other form of communication, and if the examples cannot be given from life, hypothetical examples will do. An example is worth a thousand words of explanation.

To conclude on the letter form itself, here are two further suggestions which may increase the clarity and readability of letters:

1. Place a brief heading on the letter after the salutation, indicating the letter's subject, as TAX ASPECTS OF JOHNSON MERGER *or* SUGGESTIONS TO IMPROVE VILLAGE PARKING. Such headings will give the reader an immediate grasp of the letter's substance and also greatly facilitate filing.

2. Use subheads where the letter is more than two pages long, thus giving the reader a quick grasp of how the subject is treated (more about this in studying reports). Example: *Present procedures, Recommended procedures, Conclusion.*

Let us now turn from the form of the letter itself to the management of volume in correspondence, which is one of the principal problems of the busy man today.

If the letter form is to be used effectively for short messages, some sort of program must be set up to manage correspondence as a whole. Such a program could go something like this:

1. Develop the habit of answering mail that needs to be answered immediately.

2. Plan letters, memoranda, and other routine communications for a minimum of writing consistent with courtesy and warmth.

3. Develop carefully designed prefabricated letters, paragraphs, and phrases for important and repetitive situa-

tions. Well conceived, these can sound more natural than dictated material. They will generally be more concise, more courteous, and more effective.

4. Use note pads with your name engraved at the top for short messages where appropriate to avoid putting everything through the stenographic mill.

5. To personalize printed materials, attach your card with a brief warm message.

Many a gentleman of the old school will look with dismay and abhorrence on this approach to what once was considered a substantial art. Men used to take pride in their letters and hold a correspondence with their peers that was in itself both profitable and refreshing. Has all this departed, leaving nothing but this organizational correspondence dedicated only to getting across the information quickly and effectively and in as few words as possible? Not entirely. The letter with flair and character still survives, but it must be supplemented with that great flood of communication represented by the telephone, the new mobility offered by air travel, and the other aids to instant communication. Also, the matter must be of enough consequence to deserve this sort of attention and form. There is no time any more to be wasted in vain or pretentious letters or messages—in long, verbose, or empty communications. Let us all listen to the angry voice of Aurangzeb, Emperor of Hindustan, some centuries ago rebuking a former teacher for inflicting upon him "things . . . hard to understand and very easy to forget . . ."

> . . . all I retained [the Emperor wrote] was a multitude of barbarous and dark words, proper to bewilder, perplex and tire out the best wits and only invented the better to cover the vanity and ignorance of men like yourself, that would make us believe that they knew all and that under those obscure and ambiguous words are hid great mysteries which they alone are capable to understand.

7

The terrors of reporting
• • •

"THAT YOU SHALL STIFLE IN YOUR OWN REPORT
..." Shakespeare wrote, and unfortunately this is often
the case with business reports. Nevertheless, the sound
report is the cherished vehicle of important ideas, information, and knowledge in any sizable organization.

We use the word "report" here to include both
forms, the report and the memorandum, since the two
are so similar in use that for all practical purposes they
may be considered one form. Strictly speaking, a
memorandum is defined as an informal record of something, originally a note to jog the memory, while a report
is considered a more formal account of some matter. In
actual practice, the subject matter of both may well be
the same. The difference in format is of minor consequence, since both vary even from organization to organization. The administrator may select that style or
format which best suits his purposes or with which his
recipients may be most familiar from among a broad
range of such styles which have sprung up in this
medium.

When analyzed, all memoranda and reports fall
into five general types characterized by basic purpose,
and the formats suggested here may illumine the true
nature of this form for use as a medium of communication and administrations. Before studying these five
general types, however, it may be well to consider how
widespread and useful the report has become, something of the economics of report writing, and what general techniques may be followed to prepare reports.

The late Alfred P. Sloan, Jr., in his work *My Years
with General Motors* gives a striking example of the in-

fluence and effectiveness of memoranda and reports as communications forces in the administration of a business. In half a dozen documents, either in memorandum or report form, the whole philosophy and structure of the General Motors organization were promulgated and communicated to management. While these memoranda and reports were often almost unbearably wordy and sometimes badly organized, they conveyed very strongly the sense of the new thinking; and, of course, they were supplemented with the use of conferences, committee meetings, and other forms of organized communicating and by the great ocean of unorganized communicating which goes on constantly in any management group.

But the reports are the policy-making forms to which Sloan returns again and again; and, in all organizations of any scope or complexity, the memorandum and report as forms must play a powerful role in communicating complex ideas, recommendations, and information.

In science and technology and in many professions, the report is often the main product of the investigation or work done, and thus of the writing of reports there is sometimes no end. Furthermore, many types of information reports pouring out daily, weekly, and monthly in large organizations have become great slowdown walls of paperwork. All organizations need to look at their reporting systems to be sure this valuable and important form is not being wasted or misused through conveyance of useless or unneeded information or information not sufficiently organized and digested to be understandable.

As in managing correspondence, so reports and memoranda might be programmed at great savings in time, effort, and expense and with a striking increase in effectiveness. In one company, it was found that devising formats for common reports greatly increased the quality of the reports and cut down on the time required to prepare them. In fact, in the case of their most common report, it was found that using the format had reduced the preparation time from an estimated four days to three hours, principally because the material could be dictated into the format. Furthermore, while the format saved the writer considerable organizing time, it compelled him, nevertheless, to secure for its fulfillment the kind of information that would be most useful to the recipient and to present it in the most effective way.

Thus, a study of the characteristics of the good report and the analysis of the five general kinds of reports may be useful in managing this form of business communications.

*W*HAT IS A GOOD REPORT?

The secret of good reporting lies in the stressing of three basic elements: first, the value of the report to its recipient, and this value should be indicated both in the title and the first paragraph; second, the substance of the report, and this should be highlighted by the use of such devices as subheadings or side headings; and, finally, a proper organization of the material so that its parts present themselves to the reader in a natural or sensible sequence.

We have already indicated a few of the characteristics of a good report in our discussions on techniques of writing and in the four key questions indicated previously to be asked about any communication: (1) To whom am I speaking? (2) What is the value of this communication? (3) What is its point or conclusion? (4) Can the substance be so set off or highlighted as to be immediately grasped by the reader?

There are, however, a number of further elements and techniques in preparing reports, in measuring their quality, in organizing the material, and in the actual writing which can be very useful in policy-making and in developing essential information at reasonable cost.

Let us begin by establishing three basic measures for a sound report. We do this by asking ourselves three key questions:

1. *Is the report a useful instrument?* Does it enable the recipient to operate his business or improve the organization in some way more effectively? Does it bring the organization or the recipient savings through helping to rearrange certain operations, through proper management and planning, through systems procedures? In short, does it have a value spelled out? Not only must the

substance of the report indicate this value, but the report itself must be presented in such a way that it is itself the instrument by which the organization can go about carrying out these improvements.

2. *Does the report indicate clearly the quality and value of the writer's work?* Unless the recipient sees clearly the full value of the writer's work to him and to his company, he will not be motivated to carry out the changes or improvements suggested. Again, for that reason alone, it is important that the true value both in general and in specific instances be highlighted in the report. This type of good report—useful to the recipient and clearly indicating the value of the work—will enhance the writer's reputation.

3. *Is the report effective as a "silent salesman" of the writer's authority or competence?* Finally, a truly good report will indicate by its tone and approach the authority and competence of the man who prepared it and will be in rapport with the receiver's customs and personality. Many good reports have failed to persuade because the tone and the approach have been unsuitable to the recipient or the organization.

These are the three criteria by which a man might measure all reports which he prepares—their usefulness, their value as a showcase for the thinking or the work done, and their persuasiveness. Such reports are not easily prepared. They usually require thought and reworking, but they represent a potent communications form.

ORGANIZING THE REPORT

Reports should be organized according to the kind or purpose of the report, and when the five categories of reports are discussed, the nature of the organization in each case will become clear. It may be noted that one great advantage of a good organization format is that it forces the writer of the report to put in the key information and only the key information, thus cutting down on that great mass of extraneous matter which seems to clutter up most reports.

Here, however, are a few general hints on organizing the material which may prove helpful.

Decide on the title and lead paragraphs first. Since the title and lead paragraphs must indicate the *value* of the report, this will help focus on what the report is to do for the recipient and assess whether the material bears this out.

Jot down the recommendations or the items of special interest or other material and arrange in order of importance. This will enable the preparer to see quickly what material he has at hand and to consider what further material, i.e., studies, charts, etc., might be required to make the report the kind needed to measure up to the criteria suggested.

Decide which format best presents this type of material. While most reports can be effectively presented by one or another of the five formats indicated later, sometimes a combination of one or more of these formats would be needed. For example, the report might be a combination of an evaluation and a recommendation report, viz.:

RESULTS OF LIMITED EXAMINATION OF TRUST DEPARTMENT AND RECOMMENDATIONS DESIGNED TO INCREASE THE EFFECTIVENESS OF ACCOUNTING PROCEDURES AND CONTROLS.

Or the report might be a combination of an evaluation, a recommendation, and a step-by-step report where a management consultant might give his opinion as to whether his client should go to electronic data processing, make certain basic recommendations, and offer step-by-step instruction on implementing these major recommendations. In each case, the characteristic format appropriate to that type of report would usually be most effective.

Use subheads which tell all, that is, explain the principal point made in that section. Instead of using tags, i.e., *Construction, Purchasing,* etc., or even phrases like *Construction Costs Audited,* it is often more meaningful to use sentences as subheads from time to time, as: *Internal Audit of Construction Costs Is Being Undertaken.* Such subheads make clear the substance of the section and guide the reader to those areas of particular interest to him. Taken together, they inform him quickly of the content of the whole report.

WRITING THE REPORT

The characteristics of good writing—of tone, completeness, conciseness, concreteness, and readability as outlined earlier—apply, of course, to the writing of reports also, but there are two of these which in reports appear to give special difficulty. They are conciseness and readability.

Conciseness, of course, does not necessarily mean brevity. An eighty-page report can be concise if every part of it gives the most information in the fewest possible words. One of the difficulties in the use of this form is the temptation to include in the report material which is of no interest to the recipient, for example, long dissertations on each step taken to reach the conclusions or overextended information on the scope of the investigations. There are, of course, reports in which the scope of the investigation must be described sufficiently so that the reader understands its significance as relating to the conclusions or in which the limits of the investigation are important, but the writer must not force the recipient to read of efforts made simply to advertise the amount of work involved.

The second difficulty with conciseness is the tendency to repetition of vital points. If the report is well organized, the important elements will be highlighted in the title and in subheads and placed prominently in the report. If the report is quite long, a summary repeating in condensed form the important elements is appropriate. It is also often appropriate to repeat the values of the report (using somewhat different language to describe them) so as to remind the recipient of the importance of carrying out the suggestions. But the repetition of points in the same sections so common in reports only irritates the reader.

Finally, as do all professional writers, the report writer should cut his sentences and paragraphs to the bone. Eliminate verbiage wherever possible. Give the reader the most information in the clearest possible prose in exchange for his reading time.

The second difficulty with reports is that of readability. Various readability formulas were mentioned earlier. It was pointed out that readability is generally the product of *short sentences, few syllables per hundred words, and frequent personal references per hundred words*, and, of course, that unreadability results from the opposite: long lumbering sentences, words with many syllables where a word with one or two syllables would do (example: *utilize* for *use*), and turning most sentences into the passive voice with no references at all (example: the sentence you have just read). Of course, not all sentences must be short, not all words monosyllabic. Readability is only one element of style; while reducing language to baby talk might increase readability, the elements of color, flavor, personality, and authority which are equally important in most cases would be lacking.

Let us then look at the five general kinds of reports and memoranda and consider how best each ought to be prepared. They are the Recommendations Report, the Items-of-Special-Interest Report, the Step-by-Step Instruction Report, the Evaluation and Opinion Report, and the Information Report.

RECOMMENDATIONS REPORT

Since a sizable number of the reports prepared appear to have as their purpose the persuading of someone to accept something or to take some action, often representing an attempt of the enlightened younger forces of an organization to persuade the backward older mandarins in charge to accept changes or new or different ideas or measures, the recommendations report represents a very potent and popular general category. It is also found most useful by those in charge to present their own changes and new thinking as well.

Unfortunately, either for reasons of tact or lack of knowledge of how to organize and present this type of report, many recommendations reports lack the two essentials of such an instrument: a title which clearly indicates that recommendations are involved together with the value or supposed value of those recommendations and the recommendations themselves suitably set off so that they can be clearly seen and understood together with the value of each single recommendation.

We have all been too often wearied by recommendations reports in which it was impossible to tell exactly what the writer was driving at, whether he was simply commenting on some interesting thought or actually wished to recommend some action or measure. The pure recommendations report, stripped to its bones, might be illustrated as follows:

> Title containing word RECOMMENDATION, or PROPOSAL or SUGGESTION together with value, supposed value, or estimated value of same.

Example:

> A PROPOSAL TO COMBINE THE CHELSEA AND CHANDLER DIVISIONS TO INCREASE PROFITABILITY AND ACHIEVE ESTIMATED SAVINGS OF $10 MILLION

This title is long, cumbersome, and clumsy, but it meets two essential purposes of a title for a recommendations report. It indicates that something is being recommended, and it states the values or supposed values of the recommendations.

The following is an example of recommendations set off with value and explanations of each:

Example:

> Recommendation 1: that production of the Chelsea Division be transferred to the Chandler and Makin Plants to allow modernization at Chelsea
> >   (explanation)
>
> Recommendation 2: that transfer be made of Chelsea order processing to Chandler to eliminate duplication of etc.
> >   (explanation)

Here the listing or setting off the recommendations and tagging them as such make clear what it is that the report requires in the way of action or change or measures.

This category of report, like those of at least three others of the five, is most effective and most persuasive when it is simplest.

*I*TEMS-OF-SPECIAL-INTEREST REPORT

This category covers a large number of reports which have as their objective the selecting from a mass of data of certain items or problems or situations to bring to the attention of the recipient of the report. The recipient or recipients may be the president, the board of directors, or some official whose attention should be directed to the items or whose thinking is solicited for them. Under each item listed, the writer may indicate why he is drawing attention to it or add his own comments. This differs from the recommendations report in that no recommendations are being made. Items and perhaps possible disposition of them, where several alternatives suggest themselves, are only being considered.

The key to this report is the phrasing of the idea of items of special interest in the title, such as "Situations of Special Interest" or "Problems Requiring the Board's Attention," etc., and the various items set off with comment on them below each. Stripped, the report would have these basic elements:

Title

usually REPORT TO _____ ON MATTERS OF SPECIAL INTEREST OR CONCERN ARISING FROM THE PROPOSED MERGER, etc.

Lead paragraph

indicates that these are matters to which attention should be directed in the proposed merger negotiations, etc.

Body

possibly underlined single sentence summaries of each matter or problem with explanation or comment under each. The items should be presented in the order of their importance.

(Optional)

description of general situation from which these matters are emphasized.

Most items-of-special-interest material is cast in the form of a memorandum, but if this type of report or memorandum is not organized properly, it is extremely difficult for the recipient to understand what it is about. The author has seen more memoranda of this category which were almost impenetrable to the reader than those of any other category. The reason for drawing attention to the matter may be different in each case. The explanation or comment should make clear this reason, where it is not self-explanatory.

STEP-BY-STEP INSTRUCTION REPORT

This is one of the simplest of the report categories to understand and one of the most difficult to formulate properly, since it requires a clear, logical analysis of the steps to be taken by the recipient. Reports of this type might tell how to organize a purchasing department, what steps to take to set up a trust, or how to plan an investment program. Professional advisors must prepare many reports of this category.

Basically, this kind of report requires some knowledge of the recipient's normal method of receiving instructions or absorbing this type of information, since instructions cast in an alien mold may be more difficult to understand. But all such reports, no matter how cast, should have the following basic ingredients and rough shape:

Title

indicating that this will show you how to do something together with the value of the method. *Example:* A TIME-

SAVING METHOD OF COMPUTING BONUSES AND BILLING ADJUSTMENTS

Body

each section headed by an underlined or set-off sentence or phrase which tells the step to be taken; sections to be placed roughly in chronological order in which the recipient is to take the steps. Under each subhead, the explanation tells in more detail how to carry out the step, either generally or specifically.

*E*VALUATION AND OPINION REPORT

The fourth category of reports and memoranda is that requiring an evaluation of some procedure, some situation, or some technical matter which the writer has been asked to examine or comment on. This category of reports includes personnel evaluations, fitness reports, judgments on the quality or feasibility of some project, and opinions on a problem or a situation.

The key to this type of report is the making of the evaluation or the giving of the opinion immediately and then offering the explanation as to how or why this opinion has been reached. A great many such reports begin with the steps taken to reach the evaluation or opinion, rather than beginning with the part the recipient wishes to know: the conclusion. Each situation, of course, must be considered on its merits, but the general principle of immediately giving the recipient of any report the information he wants most is a sound one.

Thus, evaluation and opinion reports should have the following three ingredients, preferably in this order:

Title

indicating that it is an evaluation or opinion

Summarized conclusions

giving substance of the evaluation; a yes or no answer, if that is relevant; or the solution to the problem.

Explanations

as to how the answer, evaluation, or opinion was arrived at.

Except for the fact that too often the reader of this type of report is forced to follow the writer step by step to his conclusion instead of knowing the conclusion first, this type of report is generally straightforward and simple. It is well to remember, however, that a report is not a dramatic instrument like a play, a short story, or a novel, in which the reader must be held in suspense and the answer must come at the end. It is primarily a form of communication, and the substance must be given as quickly as possible. It may be that the reader is interested only in the evaluation or opinion and does not care how it was arrived at. He will then appreciate not having to read further than the first two paragraphs to find out the answer.

*I*NFORMATION REPORT

This last category, although most common, is the most difficult of all to organize and handle effectively. This is the Information Report, the sole object of which is the presenting of significant information or knowledge. The great danger of this type of report is that the material presented will not really be information or knowledge but raw data. The report writer must distinguish between data, which are simply raw material unevaluated for any specific purpose or situation; information, which is data evaluated for a specific purpose; and knowledge, which represents data evaluated or information accumulated for general use in the future and not dependent for its value upon its use by any specific person in any specific situation.

The Information Report is almost completely useless where the data have not been converted into information or knowledge, and thus the first requirement for this report is to analyze the material sufficiently so that the writer knows what it is that is to be conveyed and what the purpose of conveying it might be. The Information Report, as defined here, does not recommend anything; it does not single out items of special interest; it does not attempt to show how to do something or to solve a problem; it does not evaluate or give any opinion. It simply presents information or knowledge clearly and, if possible, with style and flair.

How to organize the information and how to present it are the key problems. Here is an approach which has proven successful:

Title

> should indicate that the report is an Information Report and tell its purpose and value. *Example:* TO ACQUISITIONS COMMITTEE: BACKGROUND INFORMATION ON THE BLANK COMPANY TO ASSIST IN ACQUISITION CONSIDERATIONS

Body

> information to be segmented in a logical form, set off by subheads or sideheads, so that reader skimming the total report can get the gist of the whole and what types of information he would receive by reading it.

To secure the proper format for the body, the report writer must put himself into the reader's place and decide what it is that the reader would want to know. He can then jot down a few subheads and place them in the order they should fall from the reader's viewpoint. Then he can fill in under these subheads, and he is more likely to have an organized report than if he had first done all the writing and then tried to organize it.

*E*VALUATING THE FINISHED REPORT

As with the other forms which have proven useful in business, perhaps too much has been made of the report, but the business leader would do well to take a broad common-sense view of this form, not to permit it to be made into a fetish, to analyze carefully the need for the many and varied recurring reports in his own organization, and, in his own reports, to give that care and attention to organization which will make them most useful and effective. To conclude this brief summary on the report as a form of communication, we suggest a sort of checklist for the man who prepares a report—a set of ten questions by which he may roughly assess the report he has prepared:

1. Does the title tell substantially the nature and value of the report or memorandum and make the recipient want to read it?

2. Is the report so organized that the reader can skim through it and get a good idea of its value and the nature of its contents?

3. If the report is long, is there a table of contents or an index enabling the reader quickly to locate desired material?

4. Is the length of the report or memorandum properly suited to the nature and value of the material, that is, a short report or memorandum for slight material and a longer report for more weighty matter? In any event, is the report as short as possible and yet wholly effective?

5. Is the prose suitably garnished with subheads, sideheads or other display devices that quickly indicate the substance of the paragraphs they adorn?

6. Is the *tone* of the report authoritative and courteous and in tune with those who are to receive it?

7. Does the report possess a *sense of completeness?* Is it so organized that the reader immediately grasps its total structure and underlying theme? Is there a brief "wrap-up" summary and conclusion at the end?

8. Is the report *concise?* Does it give the reader the most meaning for his reading time? Are repetitions eliminated? Are main points briefly summarized and displayed?

9. Is the report *concrete?* Are there exhibits, graphs, charts? Is there a liberal use of illustration, example, etc., that illuminates and relieves long explanations? One good example is worth a thousand words.

10. Is the report *readable?* Are sentences generally short, with few-syllabled words preferred to many-syllabled words? With due regard to tone and the need for technical or special language, is the meaning made as clear as possible to all types of readers?

8

Puffing . . .

MOST ORGANIZATIONS SPEAK TO THE PUBLIC IN part through the form of promotional or public relations pieces, and the man of affairs should have a basic knowledge of such forms even though ordinarily he will require experts to prepare them for him.

For our purposes, promotional pieces may be considered under four headings: releases, interviews and relations with the press, advertising, and other public relations devices.

It is not true, as has been suggested all too often in our age of propaganda, that men's minds are molded largely by the skillful use of advertising and propaganda and that reputation can only be built by expert manipulation through these techniques. The truth is that most people in our society have a healthy sense of the realities of the world. A man's or an organization's or a product's reputation is generally based on a sound assessment of his or its worth and his or its contributions to the world or to the person involved.

This, of course, does not mean that the worth of a man or an organization cannot sometimes be more clearly and effectively indicated by proper public relations techniques, but the businessman who oversells himself, his product, or his institution, and who attempts to put over the pretensions to qualities which he or his organization or his products do not possess rarely meets with success in his efforts, and the brilliance of the devices employed do little except call attention to the disparity of the claims with reality.

Only the naïve would maintain, nevertheless, that public relations, advertising, and publicity devices have not been used to puff up a nonentity, push what does not deserve attention, or tout inferior products. It is, of course, the frequency of just such occurrences which have made promotional devices suspect and too often unfairly so. The executive would do well, therefore, to acquaint himself with the major promotional forms, for he may be obliged to make use of the three kinds described here: to direct the preparation of releases, to give interviews and statements to the press, to oversee advertising campaigns or public relations programs. To direct or make use of these promotional devices or this form of business communication intelligently, he must have an understanding of the nature and use of each and must neither overvalue nor undervalue their effectiveness.

How TO PREPARE AND USE THE RELEASE

Perhaps the basic written device of business publicity is the release, a presumably newsworthy piece of information sent out either under a release dateline or with the words *For Immediate Release* at the top. The item may be anything from the announcement of a new president or other officer, a new product or service or device, the construction of a new plant, the receiving of a new multimillion dollar government contract, a major contribution to a university, or the setting up of a research center to the news of a serious fire, a defalcation, a strike, bargaining negotiations, or the closing of a plant.

Whatever the information, this device has several advantages as a method of presentation to the press. First, newspapers and publications are accustomed to receiving information via the release. Second, this form presents the news in much the same way a newspaper would publish it. Finally, a release is simple to prepare. The defect is that the editor is swamped with releases from dozens of sources. Even so, if the release is from a reliable and authoritative source, the editor will give it attention.

The format of the release is simple. It usually has a head which resembles the head in a newspaper: OSCAR HENTY ELECTED PRESIDENT OF AMERICAN INDUSTRIES or $12,000,000 GRANT MADE TO STATE UNIVERSITY. The lead paragraphs are preceded by a dateline and place or simply by the place, e.g., New York or New Orleans or wherever the news emanates from. The lead then follows newspaper style, placing the important information, summarized, the who, what, why, how, when, and where,in the first paragraphs and then dealing with each aspect in the order of decreasing importance or interest so that, if necessary, the story can be shortened by simply cutting off the end, then run almost as it is in a newspaper or news publication. Releases, of course, vary in format from organization to organization, but they are simple to write and they should be crisp, easy to read, and straight to the point.

Three questions occur in using releases: First, what news is worthy of a release? Second, when or at what dateline should the release be sent out? Finally, what are the chances of the release being taken by the papers, magazines, or publications to which it is sent? Common sense must suggest the answers.

First, it is obvious that only matters either of some import or that are newsworthy should be released to the press. If an organization or a person inundates editors with items that cannot seriously be considered news, the papers will come to disregard offerings from that source and may thus overlook items which should be considered seriously. In a town or small city, items affecting a large organization or announcements of promotions, new additions to the plant, awards, and the like may be classed as newsworthy in the local papers. In the larger cities and metropolitan centers, the papers should be studied to ascertain what is considered newsworthy before a program of releases is decided upon.

Second, as to the timing, the release which has a dateline should be sent to the publication early enough so that the publication can plan to run it in the issue on which the dateline falls. The release date must be clearly indicated, as: PLEASE DO NOT RELEASE BEFORE MARCH 10 or some such unequivocal indication. Publications generally respect datelines, but these datelines should not be employed capriciously or simply to make the release appear timely or momentous. The editor of a newspaper or other established publication is not deceived by that type of pretentiousness.

Finally, as to the chances of having releases used, we have already mentioned that they are good if the source is reliable and the content is newsworthy. It is well to get to know the editor or columnists of the papers or publications to which your writers will be directing your company's releases. You can then ask whether they wish to receive the kind of news you are sending their publications or find out why they cannot use the information you want them to publish. Editors, contrary to popular opinion, do not disdain releases. Some of their vital news comes from this source, and every good editor welcomes news properly presented in this way. Nor are editors unapproachable. The business leaders of a town or city would benefit themselves, their organizations, and their communities by becoming acquainted with the editors and journalists of their community and with others of the community's opinion leaders.

Finally, your public relations specialists using this form are not to be judged merely by the quantity of the releases accepted for publication or by the number of press mentions but by their quality and the total impression they give of the company and its people.

*H*ANDLING YOURSELF IN AN INTERVIEW AND IN GIVING STATEMENTS TO THE PRESS

The man of affairs or the business leader may at times be interviewed on his own career, on a particular newsworthy business incident or event, or on his business or organization, and the way in which he meets the public through this interview may well be important to getting his own message over or in the impression of intelligence, authority, goodwill, and integrity which he projects.

Part of the unfortunate impression the general public sometimes has about business may be traced to what Richard Phelan, a business writer of the *New York Times*, has called the businessman's "foot-in-mouth disease." Listen to the ringing tones of George F. Baer, head of the Philadelphia & Reading Railroad around the turn of the century, on the subject of labor: "The rights and interests of the laboring man will be protected and cared for . . . by the Christian men to whom God in His infinite wisdom has given the control of the property interests of the country. . . ."

The faint echoes of such magnificent imperviousness and self-confidence still whisper from time to time in the business press, and sometimes a business reporter in pursuing a theme may add or magnify a particularly fascinating gaff, although by and large the interviewer is on the side of the interviewee. More often, however, the business or civic leader is quite correctly quoted, and for his horror at the results, he has only himself to blame. The dangers of being misquoted are somewhat less than the dangers of being quoted correctly.

Nevertheless, there are times when a person is misquoted. Usually, the reason is either that he did not make himself clear or that he failed to take into account the context in which he was to be quoted. There is a technique to being interviewed. Every business leader should know it. Here are five simple rules which will guide him:

1. Learn fully the reason for the interview, what story the reporter expects or is trying to get, and how you fit into the context.

   In one case, a businessman was being interviewed about the proposed move of one type of product from his plant in that town to another section of the country and the substitution of an even more complex product which would increase the demand for labor and the degree of skills required.

   The businessman was incensed to read a few days later a story which played up the move of the old product out of town and, while not inaccurate, played down the benefits of the new.

   The reporter, it turned out, had been trying to show in his story that the town was losing business for various reasons and had simply fitted the moving out of the old product into his theme. If his interviewee had known the nature of the story, he could have cued the reporter that his plant was one of the few bright spots in an otherwise unhappy picture, since new, more challenging, and lucrative business was being brought into the town with a net increase in wage income to the town's citizens.

2. Try to find out something about the reporter who is interviewing you and the publication in which the

interview will appear. Look over pieces that reporter has published and issues of the publication in which the interview or report is to appear. Understand its approach and readership.

3. Be friendly and straightforward. It is rare that you will face a hostile interviewer, and even if you should, you owe him the courtesy and candor that belong to your position.

4. Do not brand everything confidential or evade or try to conceal what can reasonably be discovered elsewhere by an experienced reporter. Listen to Phelan again:

> *". . . One of my pet peeves is the executive who thinks nobody has wit enough to find his way to the SEC files and tries to stamp 'secret' on what is already in the public domain. For example:*
>
> *'What was your salary last year, sir, and how much stock do you own in the company?*
>
> *'I'd like very much to help, but we regard that information as confidential.'*
>
> *'What was the book value of the real estate you just sold and the price at which you sold it?'*
>
> *'I'm sorry, but that information is also confidential.'*
>
> *'How did the company's consolidated sales break down last year, division by division?'*
>
> *'We don't give out that kind of information. Our competitors would love to have it.'*
>
> *The information, of course, is not confidential at all, as a phone call to an underwriter (for a copy of a prospectus) and a trip to the New York Stock Exchange library (for a look at the proxy material and a supplementary profit-and-loss statement) would quickly establish."*

It is usually better to give the facts yourself in the way you want them to be presented than to force the interviewer or reporter to get them elsewhere. If for a good reason you would like certain information to be off the record, you may request that what you are about to tell the interviewer be so considered. The reporter will almost always respect this request, but the off-the-record request should not be overused or be unreasonable.

5. Most important, give the interviewer as much printed and prepared material on the subject as you can to take away with him. Long after your deathless words have faded, the words in the brochures, copies of speeches, or typed information and answers to questions will be with him to guide him to what you actually said or think. He will appreciate it, and you will gain in the fullness and accuracy of his reporting.

These are simple rules, but they make the difference between an interview or statement to the press of which the business leader can be proud and one which transmits neither his thinking nor his goodwill. No man of affairs should fear an interview or a statement. There are business matters the public has a right to know. On the other hand, in our age of mass media and intense communications demands, the man of affairs must attempt to guard his privacy as best he can. Invasion of privacy is one of the occupational hazards of any man who wields influence, and the callous and sometimes demented insistence on having everything revealed, having every shred of information that might prove of possible interest or entertainment to the public, whether it is of a man's public or private life, published is to be resisted. It is not true that a man of affairs owes the public every bit of information it might want or that might entertain or interest it, but in any reasonable refusal of information, it is also important that the highest tenets of courtesy and tact be displayed and, if possible, the reason for refusal be offered.

The alleged practice some years ago on the part of certain publications of presenting an unfavorable, biased, or sensational draft of an article to a man on himself, on his part in an event, or on his business and submitting it "for comment or correction" appears a dubious and unfair gambit for forcing out information, bordering on a form of blackmail. Nevertheless, the business leader must accept a real responsibility to society in keeping the press and the public informed on matters that are newsworthy, and which they have a right or even a legitimate interest in knowing, and he must learn to present such information with candor, skill, and courtesy.

*W*ORKING WITH ADVERTISING AGENCIES

One of the most expensive and potent promotion forms a business leader may be called on to use is advertising—the advertising campaign as a part of his institutional public relations or marketing program.

Advertising is, of course, so well known as a social force and a promotion and marketing device that it might seem superfluous to bring it to the business leader's attention, especially since the program will so frequently be devised and executed by an agency. Yet there are overtones of which everyone should be aware.

Certain sociologists claim that in advertising, the effect is to tax the consumer so that his own desires may be standardized enough to be run through a computing machine; other sociologists insist that most advertising is used to turn people into standard consumers so that society's standard production may be maintained. Advertising today, however, accounts for a yearly expenditure which puts it on a par with formal education as a social activity, and it commands the services of some of the most talented specialists and artists in the country.

Thus, the executive who must use this form undertakes a major investment and should familiarize himself with the theory, with the procedures and practices of the art, and in particular with the methods of dealing with these specialists in a constructive manner if he is to get the greatest value for his investment and the best use of the medium. Here are a few suggestions, gathered from experience, on the ways to take fullest advantage of advertising abilities:

1. *Select an agency carefully. Then stick with it. Give it a sense of assurance,* so that it can concentrate only on giving you of its best. Many business leaders, once they become "clients," are stricken with what can only be called a compulsion to tyranny. The old theory, "Keep 'em running scared," is not generally applicable with creative people. Their creative abilities simply dry up, and they begin trying to second-guess the client. You cannot get the most out of any agency unless it is reassured that it

has your confidence, that you are in this with them and will back them in any reasonable experimentation.

2. *Do not superimpose your artistic or creative ideas on your agency* unless you yourself are particularly gifted in these areas. It is good policy first to allow the agency to make the suggestions or presentations; then to offer your own, if they still seem valid or better. Many agencies in dealing with clients have found the sad truth of Wilde's famous aphorism: "It is always silly to give advice, but to give good advice is absolutely fatal." You as the client cannot afford to do the agency's work for it.

3. *Insist on high performance, originality, and sound marketing sense.* If you do not have the taste to make an informed evaluation of your advertising, retain someone who does. The agency must be expected to give of its utmost to you. Even with a good campaign, have the agency working on another for the future, which will be even better. Keep looking to the future. Do not let your agency rest on its laurels.

4. *Follow your agency's advice.* Do not pull out of a campaign prematurely. Do not grow tired of a campaign before it has had a chance to fulfill its function. Conversely, heed your agency's advice in concluding a campaign or beginning a new one. You are paying for expert advice. Give it the fullest consideration.

5. *Offer praise and reward when due.* This rudimentary principle to a sound relationship with talent is surprisingly often overlooked. For a reason which escapes common sense as well as the common tenets of courtesy, many clients, who would not forget to give praise, credit, and reward to their own people, will take their agency's achievements for granted, sometimes make the agency the scapegoat for their own shortcomings, and too often load the agency with demands for extra services without expecting to pay for them. Your agency should not only not lose money on your account, but it should make a reasonable profit from its association with you.

6. *Pretest, test, and assess the results of your advertising as carefully as possible.* It is always important to pretest or spot-test a campaign, if possible, and then to assess its

results all along the line. Usually, the investment is too great to launch campaigns without testing them or to continue them without assessment. It was John Wanamaker who is reputed to have said: "Fully half the money I spend on advertising is wasted. The trouble is I don't know which half." This may be true, but the prudent man of affairs will do the best he can to know what he is getting.

Again, it must be emphasized that the business leader who employs advertising as a promotional device should read widely on the subject, talk with experienced advertising men, and become acquainted with the art's theory, procedures, and practice before embarking on any important use of the form.

9

Getting published: the article . . .

THE ARTICLE IS ONE OF THE THREE COMMON forms by which an executive or opinion leader can present himself to his peers, to those in his industry or profession, and to the public, the other two being the speech and the book. The essential requirement is that the author have something to say, a fund of knowledge or technical skill to display, or a viewpoint to offer, although there are, unfortunately, published articles which can only be called ceremonial pieces, since generally they are ghost written; they say nothing and serve only to place some eminent name in a magazine.

For the serious business leader, however, who has experience and knowledge to present, the article provides a substantial and useful form. Let us look at this form as it appears in commercial publications.

The modern article is not an essay. It is a carefully processed "package" job. It revolves around the "angle" or theme or point—the reason for writing on that particular subject. The angle must be carefully worked out, for it is the way of approaching the article that makes the reader want to read it. You will notice from the most cursory reading of magazines, professional or popular, that the subject matter is dealt with over and over again—the problems of the thinking, feeling man; social problems; political problems; economic problems. They are all reviewed endlessly, but in each case they are presented not from a vague generalized viewpoint but from a "new" and compelling angle. *Parents' Night in the Country Schools*—here is the same old piece on education but, as the title indicates, approached from a fresh angle.

*P*UTTING IT TOGETHER

In essence, the modern article consists of (1) an angle; (2) a basic fund of information and material; (3) a series of case histories, anecdotes, verbal illustrations, and re-created incidents; (4) a style that is readable, easy, flexible, and, within the terms of the field in which the article is to be published, colorful; and (5) a summarized or "punch-line" conclusion.

The angle

The angle is usually indicated in the title and subhead. It is always indicated in the lead of the piece. In every successful article, if the material itself is not new, at least the approach or angle is.

Basic fund of material

This is of two general types—researched and original. Researched material is nothing more nor less than the material you have selected from published works. "Original" material is that developed (1) from your own experience, (2) from questionnaires you have sent out, and (3) from interviews with a selected expert or experts.

Case histories, anecdotes, verbal illustrations

These are the flesh and blood of the modern article. This is what concreteness means in written work. The best possible presentation of an article would be as a series of apt and colorful case histories, anecdotes, etc., each making a point, with perhaps only one or two lines of transition between them. Often, the angle is best presented by an opening story or case history.

Style

The style of the modern article is extremely readable. The sentences are short. The language is crisp and pungent. There is a judicious use of the colloquial, the fashionable phrase, and sufficient language of the trade or profession to indicate a familiarity with that field.

Summarized or "punch-line" conclusion

The article should end making its point. It should do this, however, not by a lengthy summary but by a brief "punch line"—a summary of the whole theme, if possible, in a memorable phrase or sentence.

One further piece of technique, previously mentioned, becomes important in preparing an article. When the general shape of the material is clear, it is valuable to make a brief and simple outline (not a detailed one). This outline will serve as a general guide to the positioning of material, examples, case histories, anecdotes, etc. Next, put together each anecdote, case history, etc., on a separate sheet and staple the sheets together in the order in which you expect to use the illustrative material. Piece together your article out of this "live" material, using as little transition as possible. You will then have a "live" article. You will have achieved, among other qualities, "concreteness."

While business leaders, who have other basic interests, can hardly be expected to give either the time or care to the preparation of an article that a professional writer would give, any businessman can use some of the same techniques that the professional uses and can benefit greatly by a brief session with a skillful and experienced article writer. The following basic approaches adapted to the nonprofessional writer in the business world may be helpful. We shall divide our suggestions into steps to follow before writing the article, during the period of preparation, and after the article is written.

CHECKING WITH THE EDITOR

In the field of business, industry, and professional publications, the usual procedure is to secure material from known authorities or those with whom the editors have already had dealings. Thus, each publication has general sources it taps for the major part of its content.

Publications have varying lead times and deadlines for articles and must to some degree plan their issues far enough ahead to catch important issues or seasons, such as the tax season for tax articles, articles on education during seasons when colleges open, etc. These are not, of course, rigid time slots. Good articles on any subject can be published almost any time, but editors are sensitive to timeliness.

Thus, before undertaking to prepare an article, the writer should make a study of the material he wants to present in the light of its possible markets, timing, and impact. Obviously, articles dealing with subjects of major concern at any specific period and subjects which are having a fashion are most desirable from the editor's viewpoint.

Nevertheless, because of the nature of business and professional material, the fact that several writers may be offering the same kind of material during a period when the subject is in fashion, and because of the substantial amount of work involved in preparing an article, the following procedures are suggested, assuming the author has decided what material he wants to present:

1. Decide what publication or publications you would like to appear in; then query the editor to see whether there is any interest in your subject and to be sure that the magazine is not already committed to another article on this subject.

2. When a favorable reply or a show of interest has been obtained—and this may be secured through an acquaintance of the editor, through your organization's public relations or communications group's making the query, or through direct dealings—then prepare a brief outline of the article, spending time and thought on the title and lead or angle.

*T*HE MAIN EVENT

You are now ready for the main event—the actual preparation of the article. Here are some guides:

3. Take the publication for which you are preparing the article and study the organization and format of the articles in that publication. Note, for example, the kind of titles, the "banks" or brief descriptions of what the article is about and the subheads—how the subject matter is divided up or organized.

4. Use an article which carries material similar to yours or which has a method of presentation that appeals to you as a model.

5. Cast the material of your article as nearly as you can into that form. The form will not always, of course, be entirely suitable for your material and may not in fact accommodate it fully, but it will give you a guide, and the actual writing of the piece will flow much more swiftly in this sort of organized form.

6. Write the article with verve and power, holding in abeyance for the period of writing your critical faculties and concentrating only on the subject and your material, so that you get all your material in. The content is the thing. Editors search for substance, and especially is this true in the case of business, technical, or professional articles. Subjects have generally been covered over and over again through the years. To be publishable, what you have to say should meet at least one of three basic criteria:

— It should add something to what is already known about the subject, and/or

— It should provide a new angle or way of treating the subject, and/or

— It should cover the subject comprehensively and in depth.

Although, admittedly, too many articles are published which do not meet even one of these criteria, from the viewpoint of the man of affairs, it is important for the purposes for which an article is undertaken—namely, the enhancement of reputation and prestige and the presentation of valuable information or knowledge— that at least one of these qualities appear in the published work.

LEAVING IT TO COOL

We now come to that area of article preparation which separates the professionals from the amateurs, namely, what is done after the work has reached the stage of a first draft. Here in the glow of recent creation, the inexperienced writer of articles feels he is ready to shoot the manuscript off and await the distant thunder of applause. Nothing can be more unfortunate and sometimes disastrous to your reputation than a hasty submission of a recently completed manuscript. The following steps are far more vital to the welfare of the writer than he may at first realize:

7. Leave aside the article to "cool" for at least two days to a week. This is absolutely essential to enable the author to recapture a little objectivity and perspective on his work. Without this time interval, he is literally helpless in the grip of his earlier enthusiasm and the creative glow, which are, of course, essential to the creation of anything really good.

8. Come to the rereading of your manuscript now with as much coolness and objectivity as you can muster. Reread it the first time not for corrections but simply to see whether it stands up at all, whether it has substance (the most important of all its qualifications), and whether it makes sense. You may perhaps be appalled by your own writing or by certain obvious errors, repetitions, or awkwardnesses of construction, but these are of minor importance as compared with that overall assessment against the basic criteria for a publishable article.

9. Work on the organization of the article first. If material is out of place, needs to be added, or needs to be switched around, do this major rearrangement before you get into the detail improvements. If material needs to be revised as to meaning or more up-to-date statistics or information need to be substituted, now is the time for this sort of work. Avoid getting bogged down in detail of wording or construction. The substance is the thing at this stage.

10. Now turn your attention to the writing and detail. Is your writing readable? Does it flow? Are sentences reasonably short and coherent? Is the tone right: authoritative and courteous, persuasive or engaging, properly attuned to your type of reader and the type of magazine for which you intend the article? Are constructions valid, grammar passable, etc. This is the time to activate your critical faculties.

11. Now cut. Cut the article as best you can. Be careful not to cut out material or substance, only verbiage. All of us write padded English the first time. It can be stated almost as an axiom that every article first draft can be cut as far as verbiage is concerned with beneficial results.

12. Finally, show the finished product to your colleagues or persons in the field for comment and to members of your organization in the public relations or communications groups for comment or help on presentation. Consider their comments carefully. Use only those which appear valid to you. Be careful not to change your work at the behest of others unless you are convinced the suggested changes are improvements. You are responsible for the integrity of work published under your name. It should be yours and no one else's.

Now the manuscript is ready to be submitted. It sometimes happens that even after all this work, the magazine for reasons which have little to do with the quality of the article may not be able to publish the article or will have to defer it to an issue too far in the future for your purposes. You should then query other similar publications and submit it or have it submitted to whichever both shows the most enthusiasm and best serves your purposes.

The work involved admittedly is substantial, but to have a good article appearing under your name, to become known in your field as an authority, to make your mark where it really counts—among the opinion leaders of your industry or profession—all these benefits should more than compensate for even the most harrowing labor. But remember the controlling aphorism, stated earlier: An article is never written; it is rewritten.

10

Ceremonial and other talks . . .

WHILE SKILL IN THE USE OF SPOKEN LANGUAGE and the preparation of the speech have been dealt with at some length, the use of the speech before different groups and audiences as a form of business communication requires some elaboration.

The business leader presents his worth and the worth of his organization to those important to him in a very special way through talks in his own organization, at conventions, or before groups of opinion leaders in various fields. In the complex world of modern business, government, and public activities, no one who really expects to play his full role can hope to escape these appearances, and it is, therefore, the better part not only of valor but also of good sense to give attention to the development of two kinds of effective and standard talks which can be given at any time. These are the ceremonial talk and the talk of substance.

*T*HE IMPORTANCE OF CEREMONIAL TALKS

Mark Twain once said, "It usually takes me three weeks to prepare a good impromptu speech," and the business leader would do well to take seriously the humorous implication. For such talks as retirement speeches, welcoming speeches, speeches at various important and recurring events such as anniversaries and accession of new officers or a new administration in clubs or other groups, after-dinner talks at purely social gatherings, and the like are far more important to the business or civic leader than he generally realizes. They are, of course, not strictly forms of communication in the sense that information or knowledge is being presented. What they convey is a warmth, a tone, a pleasant and perhaps significant occasion in the life of the gathering or in the lives of those attending.

As such, many inexperienced in the ways of organizations or social life tend to underrate them, consider them meaningless and a waste of time. They are far from that. Ceremonies of many kinds, including ceremonial speeches, play a vital role in binding together those engaged in cooperative activities and in making more tolerable and agreeable the life of the enterprise. Often, without them, the group would find its morale diminished, its loyalty decreased, and might even experience a certain loss of that essential consent of the members of any cooperative activity without which the organization cannot prosper. Thus, the business leader who pays attention to the ceremonial demands of his role will give some care to the meeting of these demands through ceremonial talks and will develop a certain skill and some material suitable for such occasions. These talks are not only important to his organization or the organization to which he may be invited, but may also be important to him in his ability to present himself to the public.

How, then, we may ask, does one develop or put together ceremonial talks? Obviously, there is no one best way, but the will to develop them and care in doing so can result in one or two standard approaches or formats, useful on the many and varied occasions when the business leader must fill this role. Let us discuss these approaches under four headings: proper tone, honesty of sentiment, humor, and the basic use of anecdotes.

You know the words; do you know the tune?

The essence of the ceremonial talk is the tone. The famous old reply of Mark Twain to his wife when she uttered a few mild oaths to show her husband how his swearing sounded is relevant here. "My dear," he is supposed to have said, "you know the words but not the tune." And in ceremonial talks, knowing the words is not enough; it is the tune that counts. Thus, regardless of what the message may be—a reminiscence of a retiring associate's achievements, an introduction of an in-coming officer, an anniversary celebration—the key is not what is being said but the general flavor of the speaker's words: a sense of genuine enjoyment, nostalgia, or admiration, whichever is appropriate to the occasion. The message may be halting and the ceremonial talk still effective, but no matter how smooth the words, how eloquent the presentation, the wrong tone renders everything else unfortunate. Remember the key to all ceremonial talks. It is not necessarily the words; it's the tune.

Trying not to be embarrassing

Closely allied in importance to the proper tone is honesty of sentiment and emotion. The man of affairs is not often called on to make a ceremonial talk on an occasion with which he is not in sympathy or for someone he dislikes. He may, however, be called on to do so on an occasion which does not touch him deeply or for someone he does not know well. When this occurs, he must acquaint himself well enough with the occasion or the person to be able to say something good or significant about them honestly.

Nothing more quickly alienates an audience or destroys an occasion than a ceremonial talk full of bad or dishonest sentiment. It is not true that the whole edifice will fall because old Charlie, the beloved supervisor, is retiring. It is not ordinarily true that the fourth anniversary of an innovation in a company marks a great milestone in the history of that industry. It is not generally true that a group of incoming officers in a professional society will face the gravest challenge in the history of the Republic. These comments—and many like them—show a total disregard of perspective and a form of sentimentality or bad sentiment that is often destructive to the occasion. They also seem to indicate that the speaker is simply going through a meaningless routine and has not troubled to familiarize himself with the situation.

Kinds of wit and humor

A very important element in most ceremonial talks is either humor or wit of various kinds. Except on unusually solemn or ritualistic occasions, every ceremonial talk gains by having some humor or wit in it. Both evoke the pleasurable feeling of a smile or a laugh; wit generally through a certain mental and verbal felicity and humor through expressing the odd, absurd, comical, and unexpected aspects of life. Both add spice and pleasure to any talk, relax the audience, and often produce sharp perceptions of and insights into truths which could not otherwise be half so easily or effectively presented.

The problem of how to get humor in a talk always appears staggering to the inexperienced, but here is a guide based on principles used by experienced humorous speakers which may ease the burden. One caveat must be observed above all others: you must select from among the various forms or devices of humor that particular brand which best suits your personality. It is futile and discouraging to attempt so-called funny stories when neither one's personality nor one's memory nor one's diction are suited to them. It is unfortunate to essay wit that does not come naturally to your brand of thinking or expression. Finally, if there is any danger of spoiling the tone of the occasion by a misplaced or unsuccessful attempt at humor, you would do well to avoid the attempt. Humor which does not come off is not invariably fatal, but you must use taste and judgment in selecting those occasions on which to essay it. You must also, over the years, cautiously garner and preserve your successful humor for future occasions. Humor that is tried and true is one of your major resources in the ceremonial talk. Here are several kinds of humor and ways of using them:

Anticlimax

Generally, a sudden deliberate letdown from a serious crescendo will produce effective humor: Robert Benchley on the difficulties of humor: "It is not generally known, I believe, that one comic editor dies every eighteen minutes, or, at any rate, feels simply awful . . ."

MARK TWAIN: "In our country, we have three unspeakably precious things: freedom of speech, freedom of conscience and the prudence not to practice either."

OSCAR WILDE: "Murder leads to lying."

Understatement

KIN HUBBARD: "Ez Pash misjudged a skillet this mornin' an' is confined t' his home."

GEORGE SANTAYANA: "It is a great advantage for a system of philosophy to be substantially true."

Use of Others' Famed Witticisms in the Talk

This is the easiest and one of the most effective devices for adding sparkle and humor. There are many anthologies of wit and humor from which the speaker can select appropriate material. These witticisms should be properly attributed and used with relevancy for the subject. They should also be in the general style and context of the speaker's own brand of humor.

Incongruity

The placing of an inappropriate or unexpected word or thought in a list or in a context produces humor.

AUSTIN O'MALLEY: "An Englishman thinks seated; a Frenchman standing; an American pacing; an Irishman afterwards."

FRANK HUBBARD: "Now and then an innocent man is sent to the legislature."

Exaggeration

The device of exaggerating is one of the oldest and simplest forms of humor, but it must be done with some wit and taste to be truly effective. Mere amplification of the truth is usually not enough; there should be some selective outrageousness in the exaggeration, which startles and piques the hearer. Furthermore, again the exaggeration must suit the speaker's style.

OSCAR WILDE: "The only difference between a caprice and a lifelong passion is that the caprice lasts a little longer."

SOMERSET MAUGHAM: "American women expect to find in their husbands a perfection that English women only hope to find in their butlers."

> HERODOTUS: "Very few things happen at the right time, and the rest do not happen at all; the conscientious historian will correct these defects."

Humorous Definitions and Comparisons

> HENRY MENCKEN: "Love is the triumph of imagination over intelligence."

> AMBROSE BIERCE: "Bore: a person who talks when you wish him to listen."

> ELBERT HUBBARD: "Righteous indignation: your own wrath as opposed to the shocking bad temper of others."

In addition to these very common methods of inserting humor into a talk, there are several more special devices, which require a more specialized sense of humor. These include plays on words: GEORGE D. PRENTICE, "A bare assertion is not necessarily the naked truth"; self-deprecation and humorous self-flattery: WASHINGTON IRVING, "I am always at a loss to know how much to believe of my own stories"; WINSTON CHURCHILL, "In those days he was wiser than he is now; he used frequently to take my advice"; asides and topical references—these can be quite effective if the speaker is quick-witted enough to convert references of former speakers or events which happen during the occasion or even recent events in the news into humorous material of relevance to the subject—and a few others which are not recommended except in the hands of a professional humorist.

The point is, however, that humor is a highly desirable and important ingredient of almost all ceremonial speeches, that the man of affairs will study the various devices to obtain humor and try to insert them into his talk, and finally that he will accumulate over the years a good fund of humor for constant use in all his speaking and some of his writing.

The heart of ceremonial talks—anecdotes

The vital element in all ceremonial talks is the anecdote or illustrative story, and the secret of producing a good ceremonial talk is simply the proper stringing of illustrative stories together within the time limit of the talk. If it is an anniversary lunch, two or three good laudatory and preferably humorous anecdotes about the guest of honor make a good talk. If it is a retirement, a string of reminiscences in the form of warm and appropriate stories told strictly within the time limit forms an interesting and sometimes affecting farewell. If it is a welcome into a club, some after-dinner words on a purely social occasion, or whatever it is, the best material is a carefully selected and appropriate series of anecdotes or stories bearing on the occasion, properly strung together and with suitable opening and closing remarks, forming the body of your talk.

So, for the ceremonial talk, use these four ingredients to produce the kind of talk which fills the role and discharges your obligations with the most flair and style: namely, the proper tone for the occasion; honesty of sentiment; humor, wherever possible; and for the body of the talk, the anecdote or series of illustrative stories.

*T*HE HEART OF TALKS OF SUBSTANCE—EXAMPLES

The second type of effective and standard talk which the man of affairs will want to develop is the talk of substance, and every business leader should have developed at least three of these. The talk of substance, unlike the ceremonial talk, must contain carefully researched and, if possible, original material on the man's specialty, major field of interest, or profession. We have suggested that every man of affairs prepare three such basic talks, which implies three subjects within the broad general field in which the business leader plays his role. It will undoubtedly take the business leader a good year and a half to develop the three basic talks he will need for the "talks of substance" he gives for the greater part of his career, but they are well worth developing.

As outlined in Chapter 3, the talks may be put together according to the simple pattern or formula indicated, but the material for the talk—researched material from books and articles and "original" material from life experience and business or professional specialties—must be dug for and accumulated over a period of time. Once the business leader has made a number of talks on assigned subjects or on subjects that interest him in his field, he will begin to see what ingredients should be distilled out of them to be organized into each of these three "standard" talks. These standard talks are, in effect, anthologies of his best material and most successful presentations, and, although he will always want to add to them or improve them along the way, he will never have actually to start from scratch for speech material again. He can use a variation of one of these talks for every speaking engagement he will have thereafter, and he may convert one or another of them or all of them into articles for publication eventually.

What is the "substance" of which these standard talks might consist? Granted that all of them should, as we have emphasized repeatedly, be presented in the form of live material wherever possible, that is, anecdotes, examples, and verbal illustrations, the substance might be of three kinds:

1. Material which stimulates thinking in problem areas and which crystallizes and poses problems of importance, sometimes even before they may become apparent to the public. *Example:* "Conflicts of Interest in Business."

2. Material which solves problems. *Example:* "The New Science of Planning in the Modern Corporation."

3. Material which educates, leads to exchange of views, summarizes or synthesizes information, or helps raise standards. *Example:* "The Growing World of Research and Development" or "The Creative Use of Leisure," etc.

*A*UDIENCES...

When a man of affairs has been on the platform a few times he will become known as a speaker whom business and professional groups should hear, and the invitations may multiply. Whether they do or not, however, he should be selective in accepting invitations. He should decide who will get the most benefit from hearing him and what audiences he is most willing to present himself before for his own sake and for that of his organization or profession.

The kind of audiences you might address are suggested in more detail in Part III on the nine "publics" an organization must reach, but among those before whom you may want to use the form of the speaking engagement are your peers at conventions, trade or professional groups, other contingent fields of value to you or your organization, and certain educational, civic, and prestige groups. Some of the most important and influential material has been disseminated before prestige audiences through such major talks as the guest lectures at Harvard, Yale, Columbia, Stanford, the Lowell Institute, and the like.

DEVELOPING SPEECHES THAT LAST A LIFETIME

Let us offer then three general approaches for getting the most value from the use of this form:

1. Develop one or two ceremonial talks and perhaps three speeches of substance for use during your career.

2. Select your audiences carefully and use these standard talks, modifying them by change of title or rearrangement of material for each audience.

3. Try to control, insofar as possible, the subject and title of any talk you are to give as listed on a program, and do not hesitate to ask the program chairman to change either the title or the subject to conform to your standard talks. Do not attempt subjects for which you are not prepared or competent simply to conform to a program.

11

One of the three things a man will never forget . . .

THERE IS AN OLD SAYING: "EVERY MAN SHOULD do three things before he dies; have a child, build a house, and write a book." For the business leader who has a wealth of experience, technical or professional knowledge, and insight or wisdom to be preserved and disseminated, the book is the major form of communication.

Few who go through the experience of writing a book will ever forget it or be the same again afterward, for whatever the outcome, the handling of this order of material is a major enterprise, which enormously increases knowledge, writing ability, and the ability to organize and marshal major masses of data. In the business world and the world of affairs, the "publish or perish" syndrome, which dominates the educational world, has not yet become apparent, but there is no question that for those who wish to influence their industries or professions at the highest levels and in any substantial degree, the marshaling of their experience and knowledge in a book can play a major role. Even in the less lofty altitudes, the appearance of a man's name on a work in any of the three categories of books in this world of affairs—general business, technical, or text— can add prestige and give substance to a career.

Edward Gibbon most inaccurately remarked about himself that "unprovided with original learning, unformed in the habits of thinking, unskilled in the arts of composition, I resolved to write a book." Yet, somehow he produced a masterpiece.

How then does one go about preparing a book?

We have used the term "preparing," or perhaps we

should say "putting together," a book rather than the term "writing" because in this area of nonfiction, general business, technical, or text books, the book may not so much be written as it is put together. The volume and mass of material with which the author is dealing usually precludes his sitting down and writing it off, as they say. He is constructing a major edifice, and the techniques for doing so can be blundered into or planned carefully. They are usually blundered into. We shall suggest here an approach to the preparation of a book of this sort which has been found successful and which can be arrived at through force of logic or circumstance or undertaken consciously and with the care and preparation required. Let us look at this approach under three headings: before undertaking the work, the actual organizing and writing of the book, and submitting the manuscript.

*B*EFORE UNDERTAKING THE BOOK

In this area of book writing, a man rarely undertakes a book without first having an expression of interest from a publisher. The amount of work involved and the investment of time and talent are too great for the prospective author to rush into such a project blindly without a full discussion with a publisher, preferably some enthusiasm on the publisher's part, and often substantial help from the publisher in the work's conception and through a thorough examination of its possible audience.

Publishers in the business, technical, and text fields are always looking for men who have made a name in their field or who have special competence in an industry, have technical expertise, or can prepare a substantial, well-organized, and up-to-date college text. Publishers' representatives appear at conventions, meetings, trade gatherings, and professional and industry convocations. They scan the business and technical magazines to see who has been writing on what. They listen to speeches, and they approach the speaker or write to the author of the article with suggestions for a book on the speaker's or author's specialty.

In all cases, whether the man of affairs is approached or whether he himself decides he would like to use the book form for the dissemination, preservation, or formulation of his work, his first step is the preparation of a table of contents and a preface and giving the book a working title. This may seem to be a simple matter, but it is not. It requires scribbling and thinking over a period of time to work out not only the totality of the substance of the book but also the form in which it is to be presented, chapter by chapter. But let us leave this aside for the moment and summarize step by step the "before" part of book writing:

1. *Be sure to look over what has been done.* When contemplating a book, a thorough investigation should first be made of everything of any importance already published on that subject. This means having someone list from the *Book Index* all the works on the subject, also a list of recent articles on the subject. These lists should be studied to see what phases of the subject the works have dealt with, in what depth or breadth the subject has already been explored, and what kinds of titles and approaches appear to have been used.

2. *Select, study, and make notes on the more important published works out of the total list.* From these lists, those works most germane to the kind of book you are contemplating should be checked off and obtained. (Many can be borrowed from libraries.) You should note not only the titles and contents, but also the approach and form of handling the material and particularly the value to the reader which the author claims or demonstrates.

3. *Make the first key decisions as to whether you have anything to offer or add to what has already been published, and if so how it would fit into the total body of work on the subject.* At this stage, you must objectively assess the value of another work on your subject. Regardless of what the publisher may say or what your own desire to distinguish yourself in this field may suggest, you must consider whether you will actually be adding anything, pulling together or organizing scattered in-

formation, or bringing an overview to the subject. Whatever the value is, it should be clearly indicated in the title, preface, organization of the work, and each chapter or part of the work.

4. *Now make up a preliminary table of contents, working title, and preface, outlining the value and subject of the work and generally how it is to be presented.* The table of contents should be developed in enough detail to show the actual amount of content or material in each chapter. The preface should be extensive enough here to indicate the full range of values of the book and something of your style. If possible, attach articles you have done on the subject. All this should be sent to the publishers for comment.

5. *Confer with the publishers after they have looked over your preliminary outline and material, and get their comments and agreement to go ahead either with or without a contract.* The degree of enthusiasm shown by the publishers should be an indication to you of the probable success of the enterprise. It is rare that the actual work of undertaking a book does not result in really major benefits in increased knowledge, ability to organize material, and skill in writing, but there should also be some chance of the work's reaching and benefiting a reasonably important audience.

If all the signs are now propitious, a date should be set for the completion of the work. You as the author must plan time to commit to the work, and we are now ready for the actual preparation of the manuscript.

ONE WAY TO PUT TOGETHER A BOOK

The actual putting together of the book is composed of three general kinds of activity: collecting and researching the material, organizing the material, and writing the book chapter by chapter.

We shall continue, however, on an actual step-by-step program here:

6. *Begin by collecting the material for the book and assigning this material chapter by chapter.* Before writing or even completely researching the work, consider once more the form and set up, and label folders or envelopes, chapter by chapter, into which the material for each chapter or segment of the book can be collected. The amount of material required in a book is usually so great that it would be impossible or at best frustrating to attempt to attack it wholesale. Separate and accumulate the material for the work into the folders labeled by chapters for later study and organization.

7. *Organize the material in each chapter folder; then write it off chapter by chapter, keeping before you and paying attention to the design and structure of the whole.* The actual writing of each chapter should be aimed at getting the material out in the form of a draft without at this stage too much attempt at polish or style. The positioning and ordering of the material is the thing.

8. *Go over this first written draft of the book as an entity and make any major order or structure changes necessary.* At this stage, the important matter is coherence, and some of the material may have to be shifted from one chapter to another; chapters may even have to be switched, and heads and subheads should be carefully looked over.

9. *Polish and cut.* Leave aside the draft for a sufficient time to cool *without showing it to anybody.* After a week or so, go through it fast for a first polishing and a first cutting.

After it has been written...

Several basic procedures are necessary before submitting the manuscript formally to the publishers. The following steps should be considered:

10. *Observe the mechanics of manuscript preparation.* Have manuscript typed double-spaced with wide margins and on one side only of standard 8½ × 11 typewriter

paper, making at least one other copy and preferably two. Minor corrections and changes can be made between the lines, either typed or neatly written in. The manuscript should be neat and readable but does not have to be flawless. Ask your publisher for any information sheet he may have on style in preparing manuscripts for his house. Illustrations and tables should be clearly labeled, reproducible, and numbered consecutively, and the position in the text where you wish them to appear should be carefully indicated.

11. *Have your manuscript looked at by an authority and/or others who can and are willing to give suggestions and reactions. Often, the publisher will do this for you.* Many excellent additions or changes are secured through passing the manuscript out to selected authorities or intelligent friends or associates in the field. You must set a deadline for the return of any comments, however, and be careful to accept only those which seem to improve the whole.

12. *Submit the final work to the publisher and take your much-needed vacation.* It will require some time for galleys to come in and usually six months or more altogether before the manuscript comes out as a book. If it is a technical, scholarly, or general business book, reviews may be slow in appearing. No author has ever felt that his work was sufficiently promoted, advertised, or appreciated, and you will be no exception. You will find, however, that your name is beginning to be known and that no matter how unappreciated your work seems to have been, your prestige is substantially enhanced.

We have completed here brief reviews of the seven basic forms of business communications commonly employed in the world of affairs and at the formal level of communicating. The skillful use of these forms remains important to reaching various "publics" through the channels of organized communicating.

In presenting any material, the business leader should make an effort, of course, to communicate at the highest level of which he is capable, if possible at the level where art and style are important. In that way, he will produce the greatest effect.

Let us now turn to a more careful study of the various publics to which the business leader and his organization will wish to address themselves. These publics constitute his environment, the worlds, small and great, which he and his organization must somehow reach to survive and prosper.

III

REACHING OUT

Your various publics

*And what is this smile of the world, to win
which we are bidden to sacrifice . . .*
JOHN MORLEY

12

Notes on reaching management . . .

EVERY ORGANIZATION IN OUR MODERN WORLD exists in a flux of change and motion, its survival dependent at all times on the maintenance of channels, formal or informal, that enable it to reach its own people and certain other key groups in what may figuratively be called the outside world. When viewed more carefully, those it must reach may be said to fall into nine "publics." These are: its management; its employees, shareholders, and suppliers; its customers or clients; those in its own special field from which it derives its technology; the educational world from which it draws its people; the financial world from which it gets its money; the general business world in which it must play its complex economic part; the governmental and political world which sets the rules by which it may play that economic part; and the Great World of opinion and taste leaders from all walks of life.

These publics are not always separate and distinct, of course. They merge into one another; the same people may belong to several of them, and groups within them may require different communication means, but for the business leader, this concept of nine publics may prove useful in studying how to reach various types of people whom he needs to reach within and without any specific organization.

Chester Barnard in his classic study of organizations, *The Functions of the Executive*, suggests that organizations come into being when two or more persons communicate with each other and that the organization can survive only as long as this communication can be maintained. He suggests that one of the chief functions of the executive, therefore, is not the work which the organization directly performs but the establishment and maintenance of communications.

This may seem like a simplification, but it is not. Together with planning and control, the establishment and maintenance of communications lie at the heart of the executive function, and the business leader must learn the ropes well enough to see how this function may be carried out to reach the organization's various key groups within and without—in the present instance, the crucial group called management.

The first questions which must be asked are: "Who comprises management?" and "What are management's characteristics?"

*Y*OU AND MANAGEMENT

Management, the broad term for those who direct the various activities of an organization, may represent as few as 2 per cent of the total population of a group or, as in certain professional firms, as much as 40 per cent of those in the organization. Those inexperienced in the nature of modern organizations often tend to underestimate the number of those who are actually members of management and overestimate the power of the few at the top of the pyramid. As every executive learns, while the *influence* of those at the top is immense, the power to change, move, or sway the activities of an organization, even in the case of those given almost complete authority, is limited by the organization's size and complexity and by the great natural inertial force of organizational procedures. The poignant and well-known remark by one huge company's president well illustrates the situation. "The organization," he said, "is like a damn big dragon. You kick it in the tail and two years later it feels it in the head."

So, the ability of the top executive to reach all of management has a direct bearing on his effectiveness as an administrator. By and large, members of management do not deliberately sabotage an order even when it goes against their desires and judgment; but, unless the order, the change, or the decision is clearly and skillfully presented through proper channels, too often something does seem to happen to the message. Its meaning blurs; it is "interpreted"; it is watered down; and by the time it reaches those who are to carry it out, it may be almost unrecognizable. In fact, as one executive noted, in cases where the decision is painful to key members of the organization, it is quite possible to issue an order and have it drop into the bottomless abyss of a company's hierarchy with no more effect than a whisper in the Grand Canyon.

So, to reach the monster effectively, all of management must somehow be reached; and in a large organization, all of management may comprise groups who vary widely in education, background, intelligence, and experience, from shop supervisors to Ph.D. physicists, from warehouse foremen to the executive vice president. What characteristics, then, do these widely varying groups and individuals have in common?

1. Their loyalty to the organization is usually greater than that of other employees.

2. Their need for information on the company, its goals, plans, operations, etc., is greater than that of other employees.

3. Their education, experience, and motivation are generally above average.

4. They have a lower threshold for bombast, guff, and nonsense than most people.

5. The ceremonial "communication" or protocol is extremely important to them, even though they may not admit or recognize it. Prestige and power are basic motivations to any man who would do well in management. They are literally indispensable.

Let us look at each of these characteristics more closely. The word "loyalty" as used in organizations has to do with the willingness to serve the organization and in general to be dominated by its needs and requirements. This is perhaps the primary requirement for management. No organization can exist without it, and no manager can be either effective or useful without it. Generally, it is a rather common and natural instinct in men, one which has made possible effective cooperation in a cause and thus the gigantic structures called organizations which do most of the work of the world. Loyalty cannot generally be bought, but it can be aroused, not only by the pleasure of the work itself, but more often by the presentation of the goals and plans of an organization in a sound and inspiring manner. Thus, in communicating with management, goals and plans are important, and the skillful and valid incorporation of the manager's specific tasks into the overall goals and plans of the organization is one of the most vital concepts to be communicated.

The second characteristic of management, of course, is its great need, its hunger, for information. Information may be said to be the raw material of management, the stuff which management works on, as a production worker would work on the raw material of his product. The kind of information communicated to him (not necessarily the amount) and the way it is interpreted and communicated will have a crucial bearing on how well he can manage. His own ability to convert data into information and communicate it properly will determine how effective he is himself in his calling.

The third characteristic of generally superior education, intelligence, and motivation requires that communication with management be on a high level both as regards style and tone. Unfortunately, this requirement is perhaps the one most often breached. The amount of jargon, unnecessary technical language, and pretentious reporting which passes for communication among members of management is disheartening, and in a number of organizations clogs and slows down the vital work of the organization as a whole.

It may seem a paradox that the last two characteristics listed suggest first that members of management have a low threshold for bombast and nonsense and at the same time are deeply influenced and motivated by ceremonial communication or protocol. Perhaps this seeming contradiction may be explained as follows.

Basically, managers—that is, good managers—are goal and process oriented. They like to get things done, to solve problems, to reach agreed-upon ends or conclusions, although they realize that this is a continuous process, that once one goal is reached, the next must be attempted. This pragmatic and end-seeking turn of mind makes them impatient with "useless" or pretentious or non-productive activity and communication. Some of them thus become the strong silent types who get things done. They do not use communication for any but pragmatic ends and are impatient with those who do. This is the phase or tendency suggested in our fourth characteristic.

At the same time, the manager as an individual type is deeply motivated, not by money or as with the true scientist by the desire to know, to find out for its own sake, but primarily by the desire for prestige and power. For some reason, these have always seemed questionable motivations in the spectrum of human desires, although there is no reason why they should be. And they are essential motivations in the preserving of the structure and the dynamism of organizations. Thus, positions of responsibility and authority must be surrounded with their trappings of prestige and protocol. The four-window office, the silver water carafe, the rug on the floor, and the spacious desk all "communicate" to the manager the value and prestige of his responsibility and his authority and play a surprisingly underrated part in the maintenance of the power structure necessary to channel the talents and abilities an organization requires for its work. Managers read such signs unconsciously and sustain the authority they represent. Organizations which have attempted to do away with such distinctions by pulling down offices or putting everyone in bull pens or in other ways attempting to foster the appearance of equality have found a general collapse in administrative effectiveness accompanying this well-meant effort at "democracy."

There have been well-known essays in reverse snobbery in which the president or the man with the real power occupies a small shabby cubicle while his vice presidents luxuriate in huge sumptuous quarters. This serves to set off even more blatantly the "one-man-show" aspect of the organizational setup, but the assistants will often take pride in his homely, old-shoe pretentiousness and conspire in it as a conversation piece. No one is deceived. The prestige aspects of this executive squalor fairly shout status, and, if not checked, there could conceivably be the danger of a sort of reverse progression, each executive as he rises achieving the privilege of a smaller office.

So much then for the world of the manager, a man with a comparatively high degree of loyalty, motivation, and need for information; a man with above-average education, experience, and intelligence, with a pragmatic turn of mind and yet with a need for prestige and power.

FOUR CHANNELS

Through what channels and with what media, then, can the manager best be reached?

In addition to the basic face-to-face and voice-to-voice communication, which must remain the foundation of most management communication, four kinds of formal channels and media may be profitably used to reach this varied group:

1. Conferences, formal and informal, on regular and on special bases

2. Organization charts, policy and standard operating procedure manuals

3. Regular monthly, semimonthly, or weekly management newsletter or executive letter, supplemented by special issues for urgent information

4. Formal management development and training programs

Conferring . . .

The first channel, the regular conference, supplemented with special conferences, is almost a necessity for reaching management, level by level. These meetings may vary from the gigantic annual or semiannual meeting of major levels of management to the Monday morning policy meeting of the president and his cabinet. Such meetings go on constantly both on a regular and when-needed basis, and much of the work of communicating vital information is carried out through these meetings. Where other regular channels for disseminating management information are lacking, these meetings may become more and more frequent and finally get out of hand. Many a hard-pressed executive, victim of an inadequate management communication system, has cried out: "All I do all day long is sit in meetings!"

Using manuals and organization charts

The second formal channel is the network of written guides like the organization chart and standard operating procedure manuals. All members of management need to know how the organization is structured, who is responsible for what, and what management functions have been assigned to what positions. They must know also who fills these positions and something of the incumbent's background and abilities. All of this is vital information, not just as a matter of curiosity, but as a matter of fulfilling the man's own function properly.

"We thought of working up an organization chart and guide," the executive of one closely knit executive group in a medium-size company remarked, "but someone asked why and nobody could think of a good answer, so we never did."

This may be fine where the executive group is small, well known to all employees, close to each other, and strongly centralized; but where the executive group is extensive, many-leveled, or widely dispersed, the organization chart and guide and the policy and standard operating procedure guide are essential to communicate quickly and effectively functional relationships and lines of accountability. A little thought will indicate that lines of accountability and lines of communication are not the same, and that a manager may be accountable in certain respects to an executive two or more levels above him with whom he has little or no real communication. Nevertheless, he must know something of that executive's function and the nature of his accountability, and organization charts and guides are the best means for communicating this essential information. Second, there are policies and ways of doing things in every organization which should be and usually are standardized, and these must be communicated, not only in broad outline, but often in some detail and as pertaining to recurring events and situations.

All managers must be aware of these policies and procedure regulations. Thus, policy guides and standard operating procedure manuals are basic and useful communication tools in this area, and for all organizations of any size, they should be seriously considered.

Developing executive periodicals

It is surprising that this form of communicating with all management has not become standard. No other form serves so effectively to keep management informed of current material and data of importance to them. This channel also forces top management (generally the president) to keep all management informed on his or their thoughts and concerns as well as on vital organization information which lower levels of management would ordinarily hear only through the grapevine, usually garbled and sometimes not at all.

Sometimes a variant and supplement to a regular management newsletter is a daily taped information or commentary message from the president which any member of management can hear by dialing a number on his inside phone. Such variants all serve the same purpose—to reach all management on matters of general interest to the management function.

Executive development programs as a means of communicating

These programs serve more than a communication function, of course. They serve to increase the effectiveness and the potential of members of management, but they are also—and this is not generally recognized—a vital communications force. A good training program imparts to management the broad, general approaches desired in that organization; it deepens and enriches management's understanding, not only of its own functions, but also of the organization's goals and place in the world, and it may thus do more to knit management together and increase significant communication among managers than any other single medium.

What kind of development and training programs are successful? The answer, of course, must depend on the size and complexity of the organization, the variety and degree of skills, knowledge, technology, and experience which must be marshaled to do the organization's work and accomplish its goals. Many of the world's largest organizations now have management development training programs of a sophistication which rivals that of university graduate schools. Smaller enterprises may have to be content with brief orientation and new technology courses designed to help managers prepare themselves for higher levels or help them increase the quality of their managerial skills in the positions they now occupy or even just to keep their present abilities from obsolescence. Whatever the organization's resources, however, and quite apart from the crucial role played by these programs in getting and keeping good managers and making good managers even better, these programs serve as a basic communications channel through which the management organization as a whole is knit together and through which it can receive vital information and knowledge on the organization's behalf.

In any organization, management is the group most vital to the survival and effectiveness of the organization as a whole, and the manager is generally the company's most valuable asset. Wyndham Lewis' remark that "the artist is always engaged in writing a detailed history of the future because he is the only person aware of the nature of the present" has a certain relevance to management, and the key to management's "awareness of the nature of the present" is, of course, the ability to receive through good communications vivid, select, and important information and knowledge. A system which either fails to enable sufficient and significant management communication through lack of adequate channels or organization of communication forms and media or which brings about the confusion of overcommunication by inundating its management with meaningless or unselected, uninterpreted data can dangerously handicap the management function and make it impossible to plan, allocate, or marshal the organization's resources or to direct them intelligently.

Thus, the business leader in attempting to reach management must consider the best use of the varied communications channels, forms, and media and present his message with as much style and flair as these will allow.

13

10,000 working hours: reaching employees

IN COMMUNICATING WITH THOSE IN AN OR-ganization, other than management and the customers or market, the groups which play the greatest role are, of course, those who provide the organization, in whole or in part, with labor, capital, and materials or supplies, namely: its employees, its shareholders, and its suppliers. These are usually three quite distinct groups, and reaching them requires generally different channels, media, and forms. Those who directly supply an organization with its labor, capital, and materials may, of course, have varying interests in it from a sociological viewpoint, even though economically they all have a direct interest in its welfare. Obviously, a man who daily supplies eight hours of his time and labor to an organization has a far greater claim and interest in it than one who, perhaps through his broker, has contributed $200 to it by purchasing shares of its stock. A man or group of men who provide an organization with raw materials or services as suppliers also may have a greater claim on and interest in the organization which serves them as a customer than its smaller shareholders. We shall deal with the organization's shareholders in the section on its sixth "public": how to reach the financial world; and with its suppliers in the section on its seventh "public": how to reach the business world. Here we must explore the challenges and problems in reaching the second of an organization's crucial "publics": its employees.

GETTING THROUGH

The arsenal of communications channels, media, and devices now marshaled to reach employees in an organization has become extremely large and varied. One employee communications manual lists more than one hundred such devices, from almanacs through paycheck messages, recordings, newsletters, signs, bulletin boards, plant and divisional papers, and ads in the local dailies to management visits and talks at major locations.

Generally, however, sound communications with employees may be considered as of three major kinds: directly, through personal supervision and management channels; less directly, through formal written management channels; and indirectly, through informal channels. Each of these three categories of communications plays its own significant role in reaching and influencing those who work in an organization, in arousing their loyalty and cooperation, and in directing their efforts for the good of the enterprise. Poor communications or no organized communications in any one of these categories may greatly impede or completely negate such desirable effects. Thus, the business leader who wishes to reach employees in an organization would do well to consider these three categories of communications and what they require with more than ordinary care.

THE FREE FLOW OF INFORMATION

The business leader must face the fact that no truly effective communication can take place in an organization unless top management and organization policy have established the proper atmosphere for communicating. While most organizations at least pay lip service to the importance of this requirement, the value to the organization as a whole in the free flow of information, the benefits in a friendly atmosphere in which all feel free to express themselves, and the true degree of effectiveness of this approach to communication are usually readily seen when the organization attempts to disseminate vital information directly through management channels. If the information does not go through or goes through too slowly or is radically changed in transmission, the communications system has failed.

The business leader who in his attempts to reach employees bypasses formal organizational and management channels is almost surely courting failure, particularly if his message has to do with the organization and its work, for the most direct channel to employees is almost always through supervisors.

There has been a tendency in some organizations to bypass the supervisory system because, even at best with highly developed nonformal communication channels and adequately developed management channels, it may be rather slow and cumbersome as a transmission line, and it is true that it has its drawbacks even for direct work information. Nevertheless, all surveys as well as common sense show that employees are highly influenced in their attitudes and ability to absorb information by their immediate supervisors.

Obviously, a bad management communications system, therefore, will lead to ineffective employee communication channels and may, of course, actually promote resentment and disfavor toward the organization and its procedures and operations and negate the beneficial effects of good communication by other channels.

Again, the axiom remains true that one cannot have good communication unless one has a sound organizational setup. Where lines of accountability are confused, not only authority but also communication is defeated, and this important communication channel is closed. The other two channels must then take up the burden. The first step then in using management channels is to be sure that they are rational and effective and that all members of management are really imbued with the interest and desire to make them work.

Once management channels are checked out and found usable, the following procedures are important in employing them:

1. Always inform supervisors first before attempting to reach employees. Nothing more undermines the supervisor's authority or arouses his resistance than leaving him out of the communication transmission line by using other channels for information which pertains to his functions.

2. Wherever possible, have material and messages pertaining to organization work or policy presented first *through* supervisors and through supervisors only.

3. Give supervisors the opportunity to comment on and appraise all material to be transmitted within their spheres.

What are the kinds of information or material which are either best transmitted first through this channel or should be thus transmitted if they are to be effective? The following is a partial list:

Company policy
New business, new products, etc.
Changes in scheduling, hours, etc.
Good news about the job
Bad news about the job
Local changes in various locations
Personnel changes
Plans
Reasons for action, progress, and prospects
Products and services

There are, of course, others, but certainly information of this type should be transmitted through management channels before being directed through the other major channels.

MAKING OFFICIAL WRITTEN CHANNELS PALATABLE

Somewhat less direct than transmission through supervisors but having certain great advantages is the category of communication by official notices, instructions, announcements on bulletin boards, manuals, letters signed by company officials, and other official written forms of transmitting information. This category is much faster than the supervisory communication system and has the great advantage of preserving the message in its original form without "interpretation" or paraphrasing through several supervisors. It also reaches the employee quickly and preserves its message in a form he can study.

This is usually the form in which company business and

company instructions are transmitted and supplements direct supervisor communication. Such material should also be disseminated only after the supervisor has seen it, and sometimes it should be disseminated through the supervisor himself. This steady stream of written notices, instructions, letters, handbooks, and information bulletins is, of course, indispensable to the operations of an organization of any size. Where the material is badly prepared, unclear, unnecessary, verbose, or with a cold, unfriendly, or unpleasant tone, it will arouse resistance to the information or instructions it contains and go far to destroy the effectiveness of any operations which it was designed to influence.

The kind of information transmitted here may be summarized as follows:

Orientation information

such as an employee handbook which gives the history, background, and operations of the company, company hours, policies, rules and regulations, etc., or a local version of this for the company's plants in each location. Each employee is provided with this type of handbook to help him understand and cooperate in company practices and operations.

Instructional material

such as guides to certain procedures and practices on the job, safety rules, parking rules, notices of change of procedure or new procedures, etc.

Informational and educational material

such as notices and course material for formal technical or training courses to upgrade the skills of employees.

Official organization information

such as notices of new assignments, promotions, transfers, and the like; new constructions; new products.

In any organization with which he is associated, the executive should, therefore, take a good look at this category of the organization's communications to be sure that such official instructional or information material is carefully prepared, clear, attractively presented, and that the "tone of voice," so to speak, is always pleasant and courteous and gives a good impression of the organization itself. Furthermore, he might consider whether the material thus transmitted belongs in this category of official communications, whether there is too little of it or too much of it, and whether it is being presented in the best form, that is, as a bulletin-board notice, a letter, a manual, an instruction bulletin, etc. For example, the president's Christmas greeting obviously should not be delivered to any employee as an official message in this category, nor in the first through his supervisor, but in the third, largest, most baffling, and least understood category of organization communication, the informal channels, to which we now turn.

"*I*NFORMATION HUNGER" AND THE VAST SEA OF INFORMAL ORGANIZATION CHANNELS

The third channel of communication in an organization—the informal—has a close association with, and attempts to catch the essence of, that vast sea of informal communicating we discussed earlier—the area in which perhaps 70 per cent of all the communicating in an organization takes place. Here the tone and spirit of the organization as well as the grapevine type of information so essential to the organization's well-being may be caught and presented for the benefit of the organization as a whole.

What kind of information, rumor, knowledge, and data lie floating in this generally undirected communications sea? It is of two major sorts: (1) gossip, rumor, and hearsay and (2) the sound information or knowledge which does not lend itself to transmission through formal channels. Let us look briefly at them both.

Gossip, rumor, and hearsay are going to be carried on in any organization or wherever people are gathered together. The girls will chat in the lounge; the men will talk in the washroom. The softball team will jest on the diamond, and the bowling team at the alleys; and much information, some of it sound, will be passed. Here also much negative and unfortunate (from the organization's viewpoint) data can be transmitted: baseless rumors, unfounded intimation of disaster, and senseless commentary which can, to the bewilderment of management, often lead mysteriously to the failure of the best formulated program.

The executive who understands the importance of this type of communicating will not overlook the value of giving this area something to feed on besides gossip and rumor. He can do this by reaching the influence wielders or opinion leaders in these informal groups with sound, truthful, and constructive information. He can drop the right word into the ear of the right man or men on important matters which cannot yet be formally presented to employees or the public but about which a blizzard of destructive rumor may start up or may already have gained headway. By being alert to what is being transmitted here and being aware of who are those who can influence attitudes and opinions in the various groups, he can keep irresponsible gossip or untrue rumors from poisoning the wells of the organization's goodwill.

The other sort of information or communication which lends itself to and flows through the informal channel is that material which either because of its personal nature or because it touches the customs and social aspects of the organization would be gravely inappropriate in formal channels. Can management tell its people beards will not be tolerated or jackets must be worn at certain levels or that it is the custom to wear hats when visiting certain offices? These minor social customs may assume a relative importance in the life of the organization, not warranted by their intrinsic utility or nonutility, and careers have been known to hang on just such trivialities. Yet it would be wildly inappropriate to attempt to transmit information of this sort through formal organized channels.

Finally, there is informal transmission of information of the profoundly vital and essential sort illustrated at the beginning of this section by which work may be more expeditiously accomplished, a president may be led to retire, a man may move ahead or be prevented from occupying a position he cannot fulfill adequately, and other essential acts effected to keep the organization alive and growing.

Many organizations have attempted to get along without understanding or providing for any media at this third channel for the informal, largely nonmanagement aspects of life in an organization, and where this has been the case, rumor and the more dangerous products of the grapevine have become rampant, morale has suffered, and in some cases a sort of organizational neurosis has set in, arising from "information hunger" and the feeling by the employee that no one is really telling him anything, this despite the flood of material coming through the other channels.

Furthermore, without media to help serve this informal channel, the organization generally does not seem to take on a "personality" for those who give it their labor and their time or for those outside who might have an interest in it, and without some such personality an organization finds it difficult to inspire loyalty or concern for its own welfare. Thus, this channel is of very great importance to the organization if the organization is to survive and flourish amid the thousands of other organizations and preoccupations competing for the individual's time and interests. Surprisingly enough, the myth that people will give their loyalty and interest to an organization only for money still seems to persist in some management circles.

What kind of material is suitable for this channel, then, and what media can best be employed to open it? The material for this channel falls into four classes:

1. News and information about employees, management, the work, or the organization that simply tells "what's going on."

2. Feature material which shows "how we live" and what the environment of that organization has brought to the lives of those who serve it or are interested in it. This includes stories of jobs, skills, talents, out-of-hours activities, social customs and values, and interests of its people.

3. Policy, progress, prospects, and technology of the or-

ganization, which are of general as opposed to merely instructional interest and which indicate something about the organization as a living entity, its accomplishments, its place in the sun, and its goals.

4. The current thinking going on in the organization.

It can readily be seen that successfully collecting and channeling this kind of material, information, and knowledge requires skills of a kind management itself rarely possesses or has the time to generate and that the development of proper media through which such data can be channeled must be the province of specialists with talent and professional abilities as skilled in their field as those in, say, the chemical division or basic research are in theirs. The consequences in terms of the organization's effectiveness in attracting and keeping the necessary personnel; retaining a good image in the eyes of the customers, shareholders, and others important to the company; and satisfying the organization's information hunger are just as great. Developing this channel of communications well or badly or not at all may have just as important effects as those of producing good or poor work or good or poor results in any other vital department of the organization.

As previously indicated, the skills here are basically journalistic, and the forms by and large are news and feature media. While the business leader will usually retain organizational journalists—specialists with journalistic or editorial skills and background—to direct and operate these channels in accordance with organization policy and goals, he should himself nevertheless have a generalist's sound knowledge of the principal categories of these media. They are of three kinds according to the sort of material they purvey and their general purposes: news publications, feature magazines, and contributor prestige magazines. Some of the characteristics of each category are worth noting.

All the news that's fit to print

This category of periodical, the news publication, is the simplest and most basic of the organization's informal channels. It serves a purpose almost as fundamental and necessary as washrooms or good lighting. It tells people what is going on. People *have* to know what is going on. If they do not, the disease which we have called broadly "information hunger" sets in, in a special form, with such symptoms as an unusually heavy load of informal get-togethers, useless meetings, and the sense of deprivation expressed in such phrases as "Nobody ever tells us anything," and "You never know what's going on around here." This despite the fact that management may put out hundreds, even thousands, of special letters and announcements on every significant event in their sphere.

This informal channel keeps the members of the organization abreast of what is happening in the various areas of the organization's world. Its chief characteristics must be timeliness and regularity; it must come out often enough to satisfy its readers' need to know while events are fresh. This makes the paper usually a weekly, a fortnightly, or at the least a monthly. Beyond that time span, a paper or magazine ceases to be a suitable news vehicle and moves into our second informal channel category: the feature magazine. Many managers and some editors are disturbed because these primary news publications are not often carefully looked at or read from cover to cover. They are simply glanced at. This does not mean they are not serving their purpose—to tell people what is going on. Even if the paper hits the wastebasket a minute after reaching a typical reader, it may well have satisfied this vital information hunger and have served the organization well in informing the employee briefly in many important areas. Unfortunately, this news medium is so vital that it does not seem to matter much whether it is well done or not so long as it is there, and some of the dreariest, most achingly cliché-ridden prose and stories in the world seem to be spawned in this press. Nevertheless, every organization or group over a certain size should have one of these papers.

The company's show piece

The second informal channel, the feature magazine, is an entirely different type of medium. As its name implies, its purpose is to reflect the thinking, knowledge, and life of the company through features, stories, and photojournalism. It is generally staff written, and it deals usually with four sorts of stories: "stories to make you do something by," as one editor put it, in which may be included features to promote safety, diminish absenteeism, and promote management and company objectives; "stories to tell the world about us by," in which the organization's accomplishments and operations are shown; associative stories or stories which relate the organization to the larger world; and "how we live" stories or pieces on the life of the organization and its people as social units done somewhat more elaborately than a news channel might be able to do them.

Feature magazines usually come out on a monthly, bimonthly, or quarterly basis.

A bastard form of feature-news magazine often published by medium-size organizations contains both feature articles and news. This is a difficult combination to handle well because the feature material, if it is to be effective, requires a reasonable time to prepare properly, while the news material demands early release. It is better, when feasible, to break this combination into the two informal channels, newspaper and feature magazine, each separate and appearing at its own required tempo.

Feature magazines can be extremely useful both to further management objectives and to present an attractive picture of the company to those inside and outside the organization. Only experienced organizational editors can sufficiently interpret the organization's environment to produce this type of material and publication for the organization.

The contributor prestige quarterly

A third informal channel which is usually only in part directed at employees may be mentioned here. This is the contributor or prestige quarterly. Usually, only major organizations can support these publications, not because they are costly, although some of them are, but because they require talent of a high order from either inside or outside the organization both in their editing and in their content. Their prime purpose is to reach opinion leaders important to the organization or its field and to enhance the prestige of the organization itself. Material is commissioned from eminent men or professional writers outside the organization or from the more brilliant men who are authorities in their fields inside the organization. All or selected employees and usually a large part of management as well as the organization's major outside publics may be on this publication's mailing list. The range of prestige magazines may be illustrated by such publications as the general interest magazine commissioning authorities on subjects of current interest, such as population control and technology's influence in history, published by a large business machine and computer company; the magazine of financial and general business articles beamed to top executives, published by a large accounting firm; and the quarterly devoted to major political and social questions, published by a multiplant electrical equipment company.

There are other media forms in this group of informal communications channels to employees, such as special booklets or brochures on various subjects of interest to the recipient as an employee, flyers telling of employee picnics and other employee events, ads in town newspapers, or pages of purely employee letters or greetings from the president, etc. The backbone of this informal channel, however, is the periodical, and every organization of any size should maintain at least the first category, the news publication, and probably the second, the feature magazine, also. Without them, even though the first two channels, through supervisors and official written communication, are working well, the organization may begin to show the distressing and crippling symptoms of "information hunger."

14

Buying customers and clients

"THE PURPOSE OF A BUSINESS," PETER F. Drucker remarked some years ago, "is not to sell products but to buy customers." If the array of communications media, channels, and forms for reaching employees is great, that for reaching customers or clients has become even more varied and high powered. In our market economy, the intense communication barrage directed upon customers or consumers by the organization has become so powerful, ingenious, and all-embracing that many observers of the modern world suggest that human life is now dominated and manipulated by this phenomenon.

Fortunately, this is not the case. Intriguing as is the idea that we are all slaves to our gadgets and products, that the communications of advertising and marketing have reduced us to the status of materialist robots whose purpose in life is to maintain the high productivity of our economy by consuming adequately, there seem, on the contrary, to have arisen, together with the rise in prosperity and ability to consume, a certain selectivity and a hardness in our receptivity to these blandishments. With certain notable exceptions, most products or services must meet ever-higher standards of quality, usefulness, and safety to achieve our acceptance, regardless of the persuasive powers of the communications arsenal.

Accompanying this resistance to the glut of products is a resistance by the public to the language by which these products are marketed. The ordinary citizen in our society has been able to inure himself to the constant, implacable barrage of advertising, touting, and promoting. We no longer hear the jogged-up commercial, and we react angrily and negatively to the blatant, the overlong, the tasteless. The outraged television viewer who compiles lists of products he will under no circumstances purchase because of the insulting commercials on their behalf is a symptom of this response. Such sophistication and enhanced standards on the part of the consumer will probably continue and increase.

On the positive side, however, there has been a truly phenomenal rise in the quality and talent of communications with the consumer public. The skills needed to reach this public successfully require that the business leader retain specialists and counsel of a high order, and he himself will do well to study not only the variety of the channels and media involved but also what these channels bring him. Let us look briefly at four kinds of communicating with this public: marketing research, product testing, advertising, and promotion and publicity.

MARKETING RESEARCH AND WHAT PEOPLE SAY ABOUT IT

Marketing research is one of the most powerful and fruitful channels to reach the consumer, and no organization should be without it. What is it and how is it undertaken?

We may say that it is simply finding out from the customer why he buys your product, and it may involve anything from (in a small organization) the president's simply going out and talking to the customers, through asking salesmen to check and give their experience and knowledge on the subject, to the retaining of a sophisticated agency to make an in-depth study using everything from questionnaires to motivational research techniques.

The larger an organization becomes, the more likely it is to lose touch with its customers and to immerse itself in its own operations, enamored of the products which have brought it its success and preoccupied with internal matters of technique that are far from its customers' interests or desires. Today products and services burgeon, grow old, and die quickly; consumers' tastes change rapidly; their loyalties fade fast, and they turn to something new or better. So it becomes a matter of life and death whether an organization can keep contact with its customers. One of the main channels is marketing research.

What kind of information can be brought through this channel? Here are some findings of which the business executive should be aware:

1. Customers do not buy products; they buy satisfactions. An organization must find out what satisfactions its products or services really offer and how the product or the service can be improved to more fully meet them.

2. These satisfactions may be offered by other products of quite unexpected or different sorts. As Drucker has pointed out: ". . . the Cadillac competes for the customer's money with mink coats, jewelry, the skiing vacation in the luxury resort . . .," not just with other luxury automobiles. Marketing research can, as well, show what the customer is buying in place of your product.

3. The product you love may already be a loser. Products have a life cycle, and marketing research can tell you in time when the love affair is about over between your product and the customer.

4. Communicating with customers is not as difficult as is generally believed, but it does require listening. You must listen to what the customer is saying, not keep telling him what you want him to hear. Marketing research is listening.

PRODUCT TESTING—OF COURSE

A second important channel to the customer is product testing, the pilot marketing of a product to representative consumers, either in one area or through selected outlets. Almost all retail products must be tested this way first. Many, of course, do not survive such tests, but many more show unusual powers of "buying customers" for the organization. How are such tests made? Two examples will suffice:

1. A large automobile company recently tested a car with a radically new type of engine by selecting a list of consumers to drive specially manufactured models of this car for a year. Results are to be analyzed to see whether the multi-million dollar investment should be made.

2. A new frozen coffee is being sold in representative areas throughout the country to see how consumers react.

Careful analysis of reactions to such product-testing gives a good clue to consumer's tastes and desires, sometimes indicates how products can be improved, and, of course, gives a reading on possible acceptance. An organization would do well to keep this kind of communication with its customers or potential customers.

DOES ADVERTISING REALLY TURN PEOPLE INTO IDIOTS—SOME THOUGHTS

Raymond Rubicam defined a good advertisement as one by which "the public is not only strongly sold but that both the public and the advertising world remember for a long time *as an admirable piece of work*." David Ogilvy defined a good advertisement as "one which sells the products *without drawing attention to itself*." The theme of this section is that a good advertisement is one which buys customers and increases respect for the advertiser. In other words, it is one which "reaches" people in the way the organization desires to have them reached.

As a "public," the customer or consumer is a human being, not, as many appear to believe, a robot completely controlled by his commercial appetites. The role he plays as a customer is played on a rational basis. Despite ludicrous instances of impulse buying, in which inexperienced males stumble through supermarkets with their blink rate almost zero, pulling unwanted, unneeded goods off the shelves with the abandon of drunken sailors on a Saturday night shore leave, most people are persuaded to buy only by appeal to real needs, uses, and satisfactions; and advertising which touches these is effective, while that which does not, no matter how beautiful and persuasive, fails.

Here are thoughts on reaching this public through advertising, whether through ads in publications, on television, on radio, on billboards, or through any other media. These thoughts are in general agreement with the dicta of great advertising men, although not couched in their terms. The theme of this section is that reaching any "public" is, after all, reaching people, and the same principles largely hold:

1. *The content is the thing,* not the presentation. If the message is valid, even a clumsy expression of it will reach home. If it is not, no striking illustration or beautiful artwork or typography will save it. Finding a valid message is the key.

2. *True art in advertising is as effective as it is in any other medium.* One of the key characteristics of good art is its immediacy and relevance to life, and an ad that has immediacy and relevance to life has content and will sell.

3. *An ad must be built on a sound unifying idea and theme to be effective.* "Loneliness comes with the territory" was a sound way to sell men on taking their wives along on business trips and thus increase credit card travel. Finding this valid unifying idea is basic.

4. *Offensive advertising is no more effective than any other offensive approach.* Many advertising men will tell you differently. They cite the rise in sales of certain cigarettes in which the advertising was about as offensive as it could well get. An old story often cited as relevant to the situation is that of the farmer who, after hitting his mule over the head with a two-by-four, is asked how he can call that treating his mule with kindness, and he replies: "First, you have to get his attention." It has, however, the major flaw that customers, stubborn as they may be, are not mules, and simply getting their attention is not enough. Discourtesy puts off many more than it persuades.

5. *Be with it.* Your advertising must be modern and in tune with contemporary style. You cannot reach today's people with yesterday's fashions.

The business leader who recognizes these basic and important principles will be in a better position to evaluate the advertising his organization and its agency produce. Once again, he should be reminded that in using promotional forms which require the retention of talent, good and creative relationships with top talent are important. He will reach the consumer public more effectively if he acts his role of client to his agency with understanding and intelligence.

*P*UFFING...

The principles for reaching this public by marketing research, product testing, and advertising hold also for reaching the consumer by promotion and publicity. They are part of the underlying rules for the reaching of any public or individual. They include respect for the audience, having something valid to say, and a courteous, attractive manner. Promotion and publicity which violate any one of these principles will usually be ineffective and, more often, even harmful to the cause. With this in mind, let us look at publicity and promotion as a form of communication with the consumer and see how this form attempts to reach its objectives.

Promotion and publicity devices are as varied and numerous as the day is long, but they may be generally divided into three kinds:

1. *Publicity which brings the product or service to the consumer's attention through noncommercial media and forms.* The consumer who sees favorable or persuasive mention of your product in media which he peruses not in his role as consumer is, of course, more impressed than he would be by its mention in the usual promotional forms. Thus, news stories or features in which the name of a product or company appears not in commercial context are extremely effective and useful. Product or company names artfully dropped in columns in another context, even though the knowledgeable may realize they have been "planted," are effective, and, of course, finally the greatest of all media for any product or service or organization is word of mouth—the publicity spontaneously offered by an individual as a private person and passed on from acquaintance to acquaintance. This is

the kind of publicity which cannot usually be bought and is, therefore, most completely convincing.

2. *Promotions which bring the product or service to the consumer's attention by acquainting him with its usefulness through samples.* On any spring or autumn afternoon in the shopping and downtown districts of metropolitan areas, you will find pretty girls passing out samples of new or newly packaged or newly promoted consumer products such as chewing gum or cigarettes. In any season, the mailboxes of private addresses throughout the land will be bulging with samples or coupons entitling the bearer to samples. This kind of promotion brings to the consumer the virtues of the product immediately and is thus quite effective. Akin to these are premiums or gifts offered to consumers to induce them to buy a product and thus become acquainted with it. The old merchandiser's adage that the ideal product is one which you can make for a dime, sell for a dollar, and is addicting applies here. The consumer is fully exposed to the product's attractions.

3. *Promotions which bring the product or service to the consumer's attention through entertainment or prestige devices.* Macy's annual Thanksgiving Day parade and the famed salesman who sold a refrigerator to an Eskimo are well-known examples of entertainments which brought and bring customers' attention favorably to products or enterprises. Fairs, exhibits, stunts, toys, and beer companies which sponsor baseball teams and use similar promotional devices all serve to call attention to products or enterprises in an entertaining manner and thus gain the customer's goodwill. In the same way, the support of commercial enterprises of symphony orchestras, programs of high culture, and the like are often of great public-relations value to these companies and bring that essential respect and goodwill which help sell products.

So we have these four powerful kinds of communication with the customer or the consumer: marketing research, product testing, advertising, and promotion and publicity. Reaching the consuming public has long been one of the major preoccupations of organizations and one which has both served to bring a high standard of living and to give our society the taint of a commercial culture. A commercial culture with strong promotional and advertising forms and media is peculiarly vulnerable to impairment or loss of vital social values, and in reaching this public, therefore, an organization has the responsibility for maintaining quality, not only in its products or services, but also in its communications.

Our society has been pictured as marked by the compulsive consumption of trash, environments turned into visual junkyards, and a senseless bombardment of mass communications fare designed only to sell. In a pluralistic society, it is true, the noise level from thousands of organizations and groups is bound to be high, the sound of many voices often shrill. If we are not to turn into what we are accused of being, however, a wealthy slum composed of blind consumers, we must set standards of quality, not only for our products, but also for the media and the messages with which we reach this third public—the customer.

15

The sources of knowledge and the campuses . . .

KNOWLEDGE IS THE INDISPENSABLE INGRE-
dient of every enterprise. The resources of capital, manpower, and materials become the product only through
the alchemy of knowledge. Thus, an organization's
technology, its business knowledge, becomes the key to
its success. One of the major sources of this technology is
the organization's own field. The technology of oil lies
largely in the petroleum industry, of chemicals in the
chemical field, of steel in the steel industry, of automobiles in the automobile industry. An organization
must somehow reach its industry if it is to draw this
vital technological nourishment it needs to survive and
grow.

How then does it reach this field and, by extension,
any related fields it may need to reach for this technological knowledge it requires?

Let us look at three major channels: industry conventions, cooperative trade or professional associations,
and contributions to professional, technical, or industry
journals of the field.

Every organization wants to be esteemed in its own
field. Quite aside from the natural desire for prestige,
which men who take pride in their performance possess,
such respect brings the organization access to the priceless information and knowledge that live at the heart of
the industry itself. To reach its own industry, the organization must open up mutually constructive channels
and a dialogue with the industry that contributes as well
as seeks answers. No matter how competitive the field is,
there are benefits from pooling general knowledge and
furthering technology.

Learning through conventions

Every organization should contribute the time of its executives and whatever expense is entailed to conventions. This channel to its own industry or profession takes the man of affairs out into the field and gives him access to the important areas of innovation and change that will affect his industry and career. Conventions are major market places for ideas and information in their various fields. Here men with varied interests get to know each other, and their exchange of ideas and information has a beneficial effect on the industry or profession as a whole. Let us look at these meetings briefly.

They are of three general sorts: organizational conventions, trade and industry conventions, and professional conventions. The first are usually conclaves of dealers or salesmen; the second, of industry associations, such as the American Iron and Steel Institute, or trade shows, such as those for furniture, plastics, appliances, etc.; and the third, of professional men such as doctors, lawyers, C.P.A.'s, and engineers. The promotional aspect is often apparent in the first two kinds, rarely in the third, although the Modern Language Convention has been said by graduate students looking for jobs to be known as "the Slave Market."

It will be found, nevertheless, that while there has been criticism of convention activities for their tremendous absorption of time and effort—not to mention expense—they have proved to be goldmines of information, contacts, and knowledge, and few organizations or business leaders can afford to miss this form of mental, social, and business stimulus. Because of their proliferation, however, a man must ration the number of such conventions he attends and in which he participates. One sales promotion director claimed that only by rigid selection was he able to hold the number of conventions he attends down to twenty a year, representing four months of his time.

The business leader must be much more selective. In some organizations, a great proportion of the executive group and its staff attend conventions, and often the time at these conventions is so heavily programmed not only by the planning of the convention itself but even by the organization participating that the poor representative misses one of the meeting's most important benefits—the leisurely getting to know others in his field. One company president is described by Daniel Seligman in *Fortune* as having the following convention procedures:

> Before each of the . . . conventions, he and his associates attend each year, he studies the program and list of delegates. His own company's delegates are then given specific assignments—information to procure, people to meet, convention sessions to attend—so that their time is accounted for pretty much down to the minute. "We permit them to sleep," the president remarks, with a wry grin, "if it doesn't interfere with their work." When they return home his executives are expected to prepare full reports on their accomplishments, and these are carefully studied by the president.

This approach, while unquestionably useful and pragmatically rewarding, is almost guaranteed to enable the poor representatives to miss those overtones—the midnight confidence, the murmured aside, the speculative discussion over a leisurely drink, the quick enthusiasm over a personal project—which have sparked so many fruitful and at times quite unusual benefits both to the man himself and to his organization and industry or profession. These come so often quite apart from the programmed activities and the general hurly-burly of the gatherings. On the other hand, examples of the direct benefits from such conventions in the form of products displayed; ideas, information, and knowledge presented; and profitable windfalls through the actual promotion of goods and services are too numerous for elaboration. While it would seem there is no set of all-purpose rules or guide for convention-goers, the following suggestions may be helpful:

1. Select those conventions you will attend and in which you will participate with great care and for more than purely utilitarian purposes. Only attend those where you will enjoy either the company or the program. Few men can get anything really beneficial from a convention they will not enjoy.

2. Learn something about the participants and those who will attend and drop notes before the convention to those you will want to meet.

3. Try to plan your own participation so that you not only give something yourself but also have time to get something from others. One of the major benefits of the convention to the business leader is that it brings him down from the ivory tower of his own organization and into the field.

4. Arrive a little early to orient yourself, particularly if the location of the proceedings is in a different time zone. If you are moving through three or more time zones, you will require several days to become acclimatized and be able to participate with full effectiveness.

5. If there are night sessions or if you will be up late, plan to rest during the day. One of the occupational hazards of conventions is exhaustion. Plan also to find time for privacy to think, to jot down notes, or to look over material you have collected.

6. Share what you have learned or received from the experience with those of your associates who would most benefit or be most interested by preparing a report on the convention. Such reports can become valuable over the years as a means of assessing the conventions and preserving their benefits.

Learning through professional and trade associations

Here again, neither the business nor civic leader nor his organization can afford not to belong to the professional or trade associations in their field. Information becomes obsolescent quickly. It requires the constant pooling and renewal that such associations can bring about.

What kinds of information and activities do such associations offer? They can and do forecast trends and business opportunities in their fields; compile and distribute statistics on production, inventories, labor, operating costs, and other business norms; and conduct research in marketing, organizational patterns, improved technology, and the like. They act as spokesmen for the industry before the public and government, and their work has brought about improvements in product, service, and methods of doing business within their fields. The man of affairs and his organization would do well to play their parts in offering the benefit of some of their own knowledge and talent to the industry through these associations and in taking full advantage of what the industry through these associations offers them.

Contributions to professional journals

One of the most useful and important forms for reaching any industry is its professional, trade, and technical press. Here, new knowledge, latest advances, and valuable data on improving techniques, processes, and products or services are presented. The executive and his organization in any field will usually have something valuable to contribute to their industry through this press if time and effort are given to prepare the material. Even small organizations with limited budgets can tell of their experiences through case studies for the trade or industry press. New products, interesting applications, new ways of manufacturing or marketing, new technology— all can be of great interest and value in the form of articles or features in these journals. And, of course, this is a two-way street. The organization and its professional and technical men can pick up a great deal of priceless information through this press, and by their appearance in these journals build up their own reputations and prestige in the field.

A review of the various forms with particular attention to the techniques of getting the most from conventions and the use of the article as a communications form will indicate the approaches which can be effective in reaching the organization's own industry. No business leader and no organization can afford to overlook this public.

REACHING THE CAMPUSES AND THE EDUCATIONAL WORLD

If, as has been said, ignorance is a voluntary misfortune, in the area of organizational communications, no public has become more important or been sought more assiduously than that of the educational world. The products of that world, high school and college graduates, have become literally a matter of life and death for most enterprises which use knowledge and brains of any complexity in their operations. For the fact is that an organization generally gets its future management from the college graduates it hires today, and it is in competition with thousands of other enterprises for this scarce commodity.

In our society of universal education, it also gets its other employees as well from our educational system. If an enterprise is people—and this is true even where the machines far outnumber the people—then the whole educational world is of concern to any business enterprise. To the man of affairs, of course, it is of major concern for many other reasons, but here we are dealing with the special concern of the organization as an organization for the primary source of its management.

Before looking at the suggested methods for reaching this world effectively, some comment should be made about the relationship between the business and educational worlds in our society. About one out of five men now in college majors in business; and, as an occupation, business absorbs by far the largest single proportion of college and university graduates. Yet, there are many who feel that business and the business organization have not undertaken a fair share of the support of education, nor have they developed close enough channels to sustain a fully fruitful dialogue.

Furthermore, there is a general feeling that business in our society has been suffering from intellectual anemia, while the educational world, especially in the instances of the social sciences and professions, has been suffering from the lack of feedback from the world of affairs which would give life and validity to theory and speculation. The two worlds have much to offer each other, and the dialogue between them should be much closer and more sustained.

Nevertheless, the increasingly desperate need of business for educated men and the increasing depth and variety of knowledge required make this public of such importance to the organization that the strengthening of these channels takes on great urgency. Let us now study the four major contacts an organization might have with the world of education and suggest ways of making them effective.

The halls of ivy

The first and most immediate contact an organization has with the educational world, of course, is at the recruiting session, but a great deal more preliminary work should go into the recruiting contact than appears at the actual interview. Here are some suggestions:

1. A continuing contact should be established with professors and other college and university officials in the various disciplines for which the organization will be recruiting. An instructor who respects an organization can exert a strong influence by calling it to the attention of his top students and can recommend certain of his students who would find a career with the organization rewarding. Some of these contacts can be made through alumni of the university who are already with the organization, through introduction by graduates, or by directly writing to the educators. University recruiting officials will also be glad to make the introductions.

2. A good recruiting brochure or booklet should be prepared as a preliminary to recruiting, describing the field and the organization in a way which gives the graduate the information he needs. Some feel that the recruitment brochure or booklet should be like a calling card, giving only sufficient information and data to attract the graduate to an interview. Others believe it should contain sufficient information to answer almost all questions about a career with the organization before the graduate is interviewed. In any case, it will be one of hundreds of such brochures competing for the graduate's attention and should therefore have some quality and distinction.

3. A training packet for recruiters should be devised to enable those selected for this important function to be knowledgeable and to understand the principles of conducting interviews effectively.

4. The organization should select truly gifted and experienced personnel for the recruiting function, men who by their appearance and knowledgeability can impress the prospective graduate with the quality of the organization and the challenge of the work. They should be

equipped to answer questions honestly and fully and to assess the prospective applicants realistically.

5. Finally, arrangements should be made to have desirable graduates visit the nearest offices or plants of the organization; and, if this is contemplated, it is important to have a sensible and well-planned routine for having them talk to officials and make tours of the location. The impression given at this stage is crucial.

Bringing in professors

Most organizations of any size have vocational, professional, and management training courses to upgrade the skills, keep current the technology, and broaden the general knowledge and ability of their people. The shaping and directing of these courses provide the opportunity for an important and fruitful contact with the educational world.

While many of the courses will be instructed by employee experts in that field, many of the programs will have been devised or shaped by instructors and professors in colleges and universities. In certain cases, such educators will actually teach the courses, and in others will act as advisors or consultants to the employee instructors. In some instances, organizations will send selected managers back to graduate schools or support them in securing an advanced degree.

Examples of the depth and variety of this kind of education both away from educational institutions and on campus may be observed throughout business and industry:

1. A big corporation operates a full-scale, four-year college of its own for selected employees. Its 2,500 students place it among the top third in size of all U.S. colleges.

2. A big retail company runs a correspondence school, teaching 15,000 employees aspects of retailing.

3. A large electronics company operates thirty regional training centers for electronics technicians.

4. An industry association sends selected members of the industry to college to major in the industry's specialty.

5. Complex closed-circuit TV training courses have been

set up in one company's space and information systems division.

6. Art courses for their employees are paid for by 5,000 corporations.

7. Thousands of managers have been enrolled in courses especially designed for their companies by major universities.

8. One big company arranged with eight universities to provide training for its engineers.

9. A number of corporations are sending managers for a year or more to various top universities around the country for liberal arts instruction to help broaden and deepen their educational backgrounds.

Using research facilities at universities

The third major contact which business organizations can have with the educational world is that through the laboratories and research centers which business organizations sustain and operate. These provide the technical foundation for corporate enterprises, and there is usually a close rapport between them and educational institutions. About 90 per cent of all the scientific men who have ever lived are now at work, and it is into this pool that all—both the educational world and the business world—must dip.

The professional, technical, and scientific men whom an organization retains thus form an important channel to the educational world. Because of the necessity of keeping up with the new scientific thinking and technology of their professions, a great many of them must maintain contact with universities and colleges, and in large business research centers, there is a constant flow of such men back and forth from university graduate schools to the business research campus.

Often, business organizations support technical journals which also keep this channel and flow of knowledge open. This third kind of organization contact with the educational world is very valuable to the corporation and should be carefully developed and protected. In a highly technical or complex organization, it may mean the difference between a technological breakthrough and technical obsolescence.

Contributing to the educational world

Finally, the business world, as it should and must, is helping support education through grants, scholarships, matching scholarships, and other aid. Many contend, however, that here the business organization and businessmen themselves have lagged badly, and it would appear that management has failed to recognize what most economists have come to accept: that what has been called "investment in human capital," the increased general education of individuals, has accounted for a large share of the productivity increases in the United States.

Certainly this represents one of the most important ways in which an organization can and should reach and contribute to the educational world. A carefully planned, enlightened, and sustained program of continued help, cooperation, and monetary contributions to education on the organization's part should be one aspect of any program for dealing with this public.

The four kinds of suggested contacts with the educational world should be the minimum number of channels set up to reach this public. The educational world is a powerful economic resource. The business organization cannot afford not to draw on it, and unfortunately most business organizations have not realized their full potential in reaching it.

16

Reaching the financial and business communities. . .

IN CONTRAST TO THE ACHIEVEMENT OF A LESS than full potential in reaching the educational public, the modern organization has generally opened strong channels to reach the financial world. Capital has been considered the life blood of our economic organizations, and it has been recognized that the securing of capital for the huge and varied enterprises of a complex market economy requires two basic conditions: (1) an understanding of the resources and procedures of financial institutions and agents and (2) the building of confidence on the part of the public and the financial community through ethical business practices, full disclosure, and proper accounting.

The modern organization has realized that it must carry over the candor and completeness of the disclosure of vital information which it observes towards its employees to its dealings with its shareholders, the financial community, and the general public itself if it hopes to build the confidence and cooperation it needs for securing adequate capital. It thus finds itself impelled to speak clearly to four segments of this sixth area of its interests: to shareholders and prospective shareholders; to security analysts, brokers, and other financial agents; to the big investors, banks, insurance companies, and foundations; and to the financial press.

*W*HERE SOME OF THE MONEY IS: SHAREHOLDERS AND PROSPECTIVE SHAREHOLDERS

Although a comparatively small proportion of the general public—about 20 per cent—owns shares in business enterprises, nevertheless this source provides a significant proportion of the capital for larger organizations and remains a prime market for even greater capital resources. Furthermore, since these "owners of the business" are often also employees and consumers, the organization has a wide range of interests in them. Finally, many organizations have found that their shareholders represent in microcosm the general public and thus a channel that gives a good reading on the reaction of the general public to the organization.

There are two formal ways in which an organization speaks to this public and a number of informal ways which may be suggested. The formal ways are, of course, the annual report and the shareholders' meeting, both well-known phenomena in the folklore of American life.

The agony of the annual report

The annual report has generally become the principal formal channel to the shareholders and in the process has had some wonderful things happen to it. In 1866, when the New York Stock Exchange requested a company to furnish a copy of its annual report, it received the following terse reply: "The Delaware, Lackawanna & Western RR Co. make no reports and publish no statements and have done nothing of the sort for the last five years." How different today. Every year the annual report becomes more elaborate, more informative, and more carefully beamed to the shareholder, the investor, and the public. The formats are often lavish, in color, and handsomely designed, and the content goes far beyond the essential financial statements, usually including an interpretative summary of the organization's year, a sort of history of the company updated, and more detailed financial information than ever before.

The essential ingredients of an annual report are, however, of five types. They can be simply ticked off: the list of officers and directors; an executive letter; financial highlights (these would include net sales, income before taxes, net income, earnings per share, dividends, and working capital); financial statements, notes, and independent accountants' opinion; and comparative financial statistics, usually five to ten years. These are often supplemented by sections on divisions and subsidiaries; operations, including descriptions of plants and facilities; products; sales; research, development and engineering; employees; and management and organization.

The preparation of the annual report in recent years has become extremely cumbersome and may perhaps have become surrounded by something of a mystique. Nevertheless, because of its usefulness and importance, the report deserves to be prepared with skill and care, and this is generally best accomplished by placing responsibility for the whole enterprise under one professional editorial or publications man who can bring together the various publications skills and crafts necessary to the production of a work of this sort. Part of the great problem in getting the annual report out is in the reviewing system. It is usually best to have the president of the organization and the controller do all the reviewing for accuracy and policy but to permit the publications man placed in charge of producing the document to make the decisions on appearance, format, and method of presentation.

Sturm und Drang at the annual meeting

The annual meeting represents the second formal way in which the organization can speak to shareholders and the financial community. While the annual meeting need not become a circus or a major entertainment, it should not be wasted by being so badly conducted and so uninterestingly arranged that it cannot be used for shareholder-relations and public relations purposes. The important principle here is that the annual meeting be made a good vehicle for giving straightforward information about the organization attractively and presenting any newsworthy items in such a way that the financial press or the general press will pick them up and give them the coverage they deserve. The burden of conducting the annual meeting must fall on the president of the organization, and he should be fully prepared and equipped to answer questions and to handle himself in the rough-and-tumble of a large meeting, where certain professional stockholders may pride themselves on asking embarrassing questions or so conducting themselves that they may attract the maximum press attention to themselves. It must be noted that despite some of the more flamboyant and troublesome representatives, the professional shareholder has done a great deal to improve the quality and the fullness of disclosure of information at these meetings, and most annual meetings are more meaningful because of their interest.

Some other ways of keeping in touch with shareholders

We suggest consideration of six other ways of reaching shareholders that are presently being used: (1) Letters of welcome to new shareholders and of regret for those leaving. The so-called letters of regret usually simply suggest that the shareholder may want to continue receiving organization mailings even though he has dispensed with his stock and sometimes ask for his thoughts on the organization and reasons for his disposing of the stock. Many companies receive useful replies to these letters. (2) Opinion surveys. Here again a dialogue is started with the shareholder, and much useful information and many friendly contacts can be established through such opinion surveys. (3) Proxy acknowledgements. A thank-you card with any other mailings of general interest attached has been found to be a good and courteous way of maintaining shareholder relations. (4) Shareholder meeting report. A report sent after the meeting to all shareholders can summarize the highlights of the meeting for those not there and emphasize some aspects of the organization's operations and results that it would be beneficial for the shareholder to know and the organization to have generally known. (5) Regular mailings. Many companies have found that shareholders enjoy receiving the company magazine and reprints of articles or talks made by company officials that have wide general interest. A shareholder should not, of course, be inundated, and it may be wise to query him before adding him to any mailing list. (6) Acknowledgement of letters from shareholders. Finally, all correspondence from shareholders should be answered promptly and appropriately. Letters addressed to the president should be answered by the president, if possible, or certainly in his name.

BUILDING RAPPORT WITH SECURITY ANALYSTS, BROKERS, AND OTHER AGENTS

Organizations recognize the important role and influence of such financial agents and advisors as security analysts, brokers, investment counselors, and rating firms and in recent years have made real efforts to open channels and provide these agents with the information they need to make a sound judgment of the business. The importance of their assessments can be briefly illustrated by the remark of one investment counselor: "A company with a good reputation, highly regarded by financial advisors, may on earnings of $1 million support new equity capital of 20 to 30 millions or even more, while a lesser known company or one 'not properly understood' would need two or three times that earning power to raise the same equity capital."

Thus, the value of reaching this public can almost be measured in dollars and cents in both the amount of capital that can be raised and the cost of raising it.

How does the organization reach these agents with its story? Here are three fundamentals:

1. *See that the information sent out is sound and as complete as possible.* Analysts are allergic to hot air, statements not backed by valid figures, unrealistic or highly optimistic predictions, and highly slanted releases. They like to know, among other things: (*a*) favorable and unfavorable developments in an organization—honesty here pays off; (*b*) management forecasts on earnings, etc.; (*c*) detailed sales data; (*d*) data indicating key financial ratios and position of organization in its field; and (*e*) something about the organization's financial policies, possible acquisitions, future needs, and plans for growth.

2. *Try to afford opportunities for informal get-togethers between the organization's top officials and the analysts.* A series of small lunches have been found useful. For large organizations, courses in the industry and its special problems or special tours of plants and works and, from time to time, major presentations can be recommended.

The important thing is to establish contacts. Analysts prefer to deal with top officials directly rather than through public relations departments, and it is to the benefit of both to get to know each other. Furthermore, their assessment of the organization's management plays a large part in their judgment of the organization's prospects.

3. *Keep the contacts alive.* The lunches or meetings should be repeated at reasonable time intervals. The contact should not be allowed to lapse to be revived only when financing becomes urgent.

*W*HERE SOME OF THE MONEY IS: BIG INVESTORS, BANKS, INSURANCE COMPANIES, AND FOUNDATIONS

Here again the organization will do well to establish and maintain contacts with the nation's major institutional investors. These contacts are usually made through the ordinary course of using some of the services of such institutions: banking services of a major bank or insurance coverage of a major insurance company, brokerage services, financial advice, and the like. These are valuable and fruitful contacts for any business organization, and they should be cherished by top officials of the company. Much of business is conducted through personal acquaintanceship, and this is particularly true where trust and confidence are major factors in the transactions. The ties in this area cannot be maintained by any campaign or deliberate approach, although mailings which would be helpful to officials of these institutions should sometimes be sent with a warm personal note. These ties are more personal and informal and depend for their maintenance on personal approaches, lunches, chats, and sometimes business meetings.

*B*EING STRAIGHT WITH THE FINANCIAL PRESS

The fourth and one of the most powerful channels for reaching the financial world is the financial press. No channel is

more valuable as a means of establishing a sound and pro-
gressive reputation for an organization both in and outside
the financial world. The financial press consists of five general kinds of media: the financial pages and columns of the
daily press; business and financial magazines (there are only
about twenty of these of national scope); trade and industry
magazines, already discussed as channels to reach the organization's own industry; market letters and investment
service letters; and, of course, statistical services. All these
media should be reached. Here are the basics in any such
program:

1. Retain, if possible, someone who has worked for the
   financial press and who has extensive contacts in this
   field to prepare the material and keep open these media.

2. Study examples of each of these media and understand
   thoroughly the kind of material they publish.

3. Give your financial relations expert the opportunity to
   develop the kind of material required for this press, and,
   as you would with all such experts, avail yourself of his
   advice on the amount and kind of data and on timing.

4. Have your financial relations expert introduce you to
   some of the important contacts in this field, so that on
   questions of major importance or that are immediately
   newsworthy, these men can call you directly, if they
   wish. Also, be available for interviews or to answer
   questions from men in this field.

Most business organizations of any size have kept open their
channels to the financial world with some skill and success.
The business leader directing the smaller organization, however, might consider increasing the attention his organization
gives to this vital public.

*W*HAT DOES THE BUSINESS COMMUNITY HAVE TO SAY?

We have indicated that an organization's publics tend to
overlap, and this is particularly true in the case of the great
and varied world of business itself. Contemplated as a "pub-

lic," this broad sphere includes two of the publics we have already discussed—the organization's own industry and the financial world—but it goes far beyond these and embraces the whole complex of our private economy.

The private economy, the term which we may find very useful here in describing the business world and business enterprise in our society, and the public economy, the government sector of our society, which we shall deal with as an organization's public in the next section, make up the whole economy of our society, and the business leader and his organization have a very substantial stake in both. The business leader's own thinking and the operations of his organization may be very useful to the private economy in three major areas: in the development of the science and art of management; in the relationship between business and the whole economy, public and private; and in any contributions to business as an international tool to raise the world's standard of living.

To the business executive of a small local enterprise, these areas may seem to be far from his concerns and interests and areas to which he need pay little attention. Nothing could be further from the truth. First of all, if his business is to survive and grow, the art of management will concern him deeply, and modern concepts and approaches to planning, setting goals, allocating resources, using new technology (like the computer), and getting things done through people may mean life or death to his organization.

Second, he has a deep and continuing concern with the order of values our society sets, since this order of values will determine whether the kind of goods or services he provides are to be produced and vended in the private economy or in the public sector; whether, if they are to be produced in the private sector, their production and vending are to be heavily or lightly regulated; and what order of values and prestige the goods or services and the function of producing them will have.

A business leader, unaware of such values, impervious to the fluctuations of fashion and the winds of change affecting the business world, will find himself not just making buggy whips in an automobile factory but perhaps explaining his business practices to an unsympathetic Congressional committee or an outraged consumer's organization. One can sympathize with the rugged individualist's anguish and defiance at the loss of some of his old prerogatives, but like spectres over every business leader and over every business enterprise stand the public good and public values, and society is quite deaf to the claims of ancient "rights" it no longer wishes to bestow.

Finally, we live in a world where half the people are illiterate and three-quarters are poor. These are problems for education and business throughout the world. They are eminently education's and business's problems in the world's richest, most productive economy, and any business leader who does not give some thought to international business and the international economy and what he or his organization can contribute here, either in the way of business or through business associations, is jeopardizing his and his country's future influence and present responsibilities in the world. Let us look at these three areas more closely.

Sharing experience in the art and science of management

There are six channels and forms by which the business world may be reached with worthwhile contributions in the field of management:

1. Through "experience" or technical articles in the trade and business press

2. Through talks before business groups and business associations

3. Through books in the business leader's field of competence

4. Through participation in industry or business panels on such subjects as automation, international organizations, new techniques in management, and the like

5. Through lectures and instruction at graduate schools of business

6. Through research and management technique bulletins for use by business, industry, and education

Even a small organization can offer useful "experience" material through one or another of these channels. Business leaders must provide the feedback for new experiments in the art of management and must be always alert to new thinking in the art which emanates from business schools and from the various industries and professions. And, finally, it must make available knowledge and techniques gained through its own efforts.

You as part of the market enterprise system

Our open society has tended to favor private or market enterprise and to trust to this private sector, called the market place, a large measure of the power to set values and allocate resources. This favor has kept great areas of enterprise such as railroads, the telephone system, and great resources such as steel and coal, which in some societies have been allocated to the public or government sector, in the hands of business leaders and men of affairs, and by and large they appear to have wielded this power and discharged these functions well.

Of recent years, the need for central planning, as well as the means for such planning afforded by information retrieval and analysis through use of the computer, and the increased usefulness of relating individual industries to the whole economy have tended to transfer some of this authority to direct the economy into the public sector. No group of leaders likes to see any of its established prerogatives and activities eroded or curtailed, no matter what the alleged necessity, and in the last decade there has thus been a certain moral fervor to, as the phrase goes, "protect our private enterprise system and the American way of life, and stem the advance of socialism and its Communistic practices." It was honestly felt that increasing the government's share in the direction of the economy and diminishing or regulating the market share was morally reprehensible and would lead to a powerful central government, which would grow more tyrannical and less responsive to the needs of the economy; thus, the productiveness of the economy would be impaired, and the freedom of action and the benefits of diversity and competition would be lost.

The case for market enterprise, because of its enormous consumer productiveness, has apparently seemed to the public to be a good one; and, in general, our society continues to allocate a very high scale of values to the private sector as contrasted with the government's planning and direction of the economy. Nevertheless, as sociologists have pointed out, while there may be much merit in private enterprise's contentions, the moral fervor tends to be ineffective, since one form of economic direction may seem as good as another to the public, depending upon how well it works in that society and how well it achieves the values that society has set. In Sweden and other countries, the Socialistic form of government or public-directed economy appears to satisfy the people and achieve a good standard of living. In these societies, a high premium is placed on certain social services, while in our society, the great prestige which the private sector enjoys has led, as economists and sociologists have repeatedly pointed out, to some economic anomalies.

In our society, the work government does for the economy—police protection, building roads, public education, the delivery of mail, and so on—is considered a drain on the economy and nonproductive simply because the public sector or government directs these activities, while the making of toothpaste or hula hoops is considered productive and an economic asset simply because it is directed by the market. All of this appears senseless to economists in other societies, and it is important for the man of affairs to be aware of such different ways of setting values.

Nevertheless, the market sector remains and will probably continue to remain powerful and highly valued and thus keep its prerogatives, as long as business leaders and men of affairs make their indispensable contributions to the public good. To do this, they and their organizations, whether large or small, must play their full part for that public we call the business world, and little purpose has been served in expending their energies on empty ideological jeremiads about the encroachment of the public sector on the old prerogatives of the private economy. The needs of society will be served. The clock will not turn backward. Whatever the private sector shows it can do better, it will be given to do. But this requires that business leaders expand the effectiveness of the business world, make thoughtful and constructive contributions to the private economy in its relations with government, and help the government sector become increasingly sensitive to the economic effects of its guidelines.

The market economy can and should emphasize its remarkable efficiency, creativity, and productiveness. A much more careful study of the implications of its part in the direction of the economy is required. Its leaders must play their full role, not as lobbyists for their private interests, but as influential citizens concerned about the welfare of the society as a whole.

You as part of international business

The man of affairs and the business leader may justly be proud of the enormous success of this private sector's productivity. The material wealth and prosperity it has brought our society has created throughout the world, even amid the great diversity of societies and values, a general agreement that this ability to produce wealth is a good worth emulating, and if it had done nothing else except make peace and prosperity appear desirable and possible and a high general and individual standard of living a reasonable expectation, it would still have made a vast contribution to world stability and order. But business, business leaders, and men of affairs have an even greater, more urgent contribution to make to the world economy: they can export technology, and they can use the great international corporation to assist in knitting the world together. This was well expressed in the words of one business leader, Thomas J. Watson, Jr.:

> The multinational corporation, the most efficient tool for generating wealth the world has ever known, can be a mechanism to help raise the living standards in underdeveloped nations. Individuals are most effective in their own cultures but ideas, plans and machines work in one place just about as well as in another. People want just about the same things everywhere—dignity, recognition for their work, some security for their families, a feeling they are doing something that counts. We, and companies

like us, have already been operating a kind of one-world system—and it works. . . .

Through the multinational corporation, we can transfer capital. We can transplant technology. We can disseminate knowledge. We can build understanding. Since we can do this, I believe morally we must. The issue is survival. Unless the world thrives, there can be no stability. . . .

This is one way of communicating with the world economy. There are others which the responsible business leader must explore. He must, both as an individual and through his organization, encourage study and understanding of different cultures and their material needs and wants. He must, if he can, become a world traveler, an ambassador of world enterprise as one of the ways of achieving an agreed-upon good: world prosperity. He must urge his associations to become international in scope and to keep their members abreast of the developments and needs of other economies. He must explore and, if he can, contribute to the store of knowledge and theory on economics and sociology.

The business leader can no longer be content to be an economic force in the private economy; he must become a social and an intellectual force, not just in the business community, but also in the nation and in the world. Only then will he be showing the kind of leadership which will make his particular abilities and skills a force in a changing world order which desperately needs them.

17

Reaching the government and the world at large . . .

BUSINESS LEADERS AND MEN OF AFFAIRS AND their organizations are only now entering upon a constructive role in their relations with one of their largest, most crucial publics, the government. As pointed out earlier, there has been in recent years increased competition between the leaders of the business world and those of the bureaus of the public sector for the direction of the economy.

Very few organizations now consider it not their business to help solve the nation's problems but only to produce and sell goods, and no business leader who wishes to retain any influence even in his own industry possesses such a simplistic philosophy. Men of affairs are aware that the preservation of the private sector's influence will depend upon their intelligent participation in public affairs and social problems. Not that this is or should be the only consideration in their attempting to reach this public.

While the tides of public opinion ebb and flow for the executive and business leader as for most of our leaders and institutions and the business world has lately fallen lower in public esteem as it does from time to time because of corporate scandals or recessions, nevertheless, business leaders have enjoyed and will continue in the future to enjoy prestige and influence in our society, and they owe society as a whole a concern for the common welfare quite apart from any enlightened self-interest. In dealing with government as a public, therefore, they have an obligation to reach and play constructive roles as private citizens, as business leaders, and as leaders of organizations, and the organizations themselves can play a constructive part also. Let us look at three beneficial ways of speaking to the public sector: as a private citizen, as a business leader, and through a public affairs program devised for the organization.

Reaching the Public Sector as a Private Citizen

The most effective and constructive way a business leader can reach the public sector is through service in the many civic and political volunteer groups as a private citizen:

1. He can serve on civic or political committees in his town, his state, or at the national level.

2. He can volunteer his special skills in an advisory capacity on public works projects—roads, waterways, and in bodies of citizens such as those gathered at White House Conferences to discuss problems affecting the nation and the world.

3. He can organize groups or join groups to carry out socially desirable projects, such as preservation of natural resources, increased transportation safety, cleansing the country's air and waterways, and the like.

All of these contributions of a man's time and energy for the public good give his voice power and influence in the way in which the government will direct the economy. He will have a say in policies and procedures to which he has made these contributions, and he will be listened to by those who are responsible for decisions in the public sector.

Reaching the Public Sector as a Business Leader

The man of affairs in his role as business leader can reach the public sector in the following ways:

1. He can join with other business leaders and associations

to help the government carry out important economic and social projects in defense, dams, roads, poverty programs, education, and the like, bringing to bear management abilities and skills where badly needed.

2. He can heed the call to government service in vital areas where his special abilities would further the interests of the nation and the world.

3. He can get to know and understand the problems of political and social leaders. Too often, the man of affairs has stood aside and leveled (often well-deserved) criticism at directors of bureaus and government leaders in the public sector without knowing the men themselves or studying their problems. Too often, we in business have placed ourselves in the posture of ungracious harassers and denigrators of men struggling with immense and complex social burdens. Some of us may not agree with the means or techniques used to gain these social goods, but we can offer alternatives and our own skills and encouragement toward achieving them.

ORGANIZED PUBLIC AFFAIRS PROGRAMS

A third approach to reaching the public sector has been through the organization of public affairs programs in behalf of the company or association. These programs embrace such activities as relations with legislators, Political Action Committees, political and economic education, and community relations and corporate philanthropy. The following are typical facets of a public affairs program for an organization.

Legislative relations

Many organizations maintain representatives in Washington and in the capitals of the states in which they do business. These representatives help the organization keep abreast of legislation affecting its business and provide contacts with the government branches to which the organization might prove helpful and the interests of which concern the organization itself.

Political action committees

While corporate political contributions and expenditures for federal elections are illegal, a corporation may form a Political Action Committee (PAC) as a separate entity and these entities can make political contributions under strict regulations as to size of contribution, method of accounting for contributions and reporting requirements.

Political and economic education

Many organizations have found that there is a hunger for knowledge about politics and economics. People in the organization often play their parts as citizens without understanding legislative, political, or economic principles and practices in our and other societies. Wherever a well-presented, objective, and significant course has been given in these subjects, the response has been remarkable. One bank sponsored a course in economics taught by a well-known university professor. The response was so great that there was a three-year waiting list for the classes.

The courses, whether on politics or economics, must, however, be objective and significant. They should not be grinding anyone's ax or representing only one viewpoint. They should be taught by qualified teachers, generally drawn from the academic world, and should be in depth, not simplified pap. Courses which are obviously slanted or which attempt to present only the organization's viewpoint usually have no appeal and tend to discredit the organization.

Other devices for keeping an organization's people aware in these fields are a newsletter objectively summarizing significant economic and political trends, articles or features in the organization's feature magazine on these subjects, and talks by visiting authorities.

You and community affairs

Most organizations of any size now give money and the time of their executives and specialists to community affairs in the communities in which they have plants and offices. They also encourage their people to serve in community groups, to sit on school boards, help administer the Community Chest, and the like.

What are the issues and interests, then, which concern these public affairs programs? They are likely to cover a wide variety of national and local areas, including legislative measures at both the national and state level which affect the organization's interests; taxation; welfare costs; governmental regulation of prices and wages; banking; antitrust activities; international investment; labor union power; government spending; and inflation. On the local level, the program usually includes attention to such areas as zoning, traffic, air and water pollution, and flood control.

Where the public affairs program is well conceived and carefully administered, it is beneficial to the company, to the community, and to society. It is the organization taking seriously many of its obligations to society and reaching in a constructive manner one of its most important and vital publics, government.

The business leader can thus play this role fully, first, as a private citizen, second, as a leader in the business world and, third, through a well-conceived public affairs program for his organization.

*T*HE OPINION LEADER AND THE WORLD AT LARGE

Leaders worthy of the name [John W. Gardner wrote] whether they are university presidents or senators, corporation executives or newspaper editors, school superintendents or governors, contribute to the continuing definition and articulation of the most cherished values of our society. ... They have a significant role in creating the state of mind that is the society. They can serve as symbols of the moral unity of the society. They can express the values that hold the society together. Most important, they can conceive and articulate goals that lift people out of their petty preoccupations, carry them above the conflicts that tear a society apart, and unite them in the pursuit of objectives worthy of their best efforts.

In the eighteenth century, the world of power, of opinion and taste leaders, of those who counted was known as the Great World. That was where the action was. That was where the ideas and thinking and significant trends arose. That was where a man had to turn if he were to get anything done or put across any important enterprise. That was where the leaders were. This Great World had its power centers in the courts of kings and in the great capitals of Europe. Its principals were generally known to each other, and they were generally born to the rights and privileges of the Great World, although remarkable abilities and achievements, such as those of great artists and thinkers, great military leaders and fantastic personalities, might gain entry. This was the Establishment when our Western society was younger. This was where any person or any organization would have had to turn to achieve fully its purposes. And this is the kind of public— the world of leaders—which an organization today must reach if it is to achieve its widest objectives. But how different is the Great World, this world of leaders, of our time!

For, in our society, leadership is very widespread and diverse, and it comprises not a tiny caste of privileged men who through birth and tradition dominate the prestige, the goods, and the activities of society, but a broad spectrum of people of every walk of life, relatively few of whom are known to each other and who exercise their influence in a myriad of different ways. Sociologists have estimated that some 20 per cent of those in an open society like ours can be ranked as opinion leaders. While in our society education seems to be the most generally followed road to social privilege and influence, opinion and taste leaders can be found in every kind of calling and station in life. The village postmaster may be an opinion leader in his community and so may the corner druggist. It some cities, the mayor may have less influence than the president of the principal bank. In the nation and the world, the great opinion leaders may be a gentle physicist, the premier of one of the great powers, a private citizen, and the Secretary of State. None of them necessarily knows the others personally.

Thus, the Great World, as we might use this term today, would consist of hundreds of thousands of opinion and taste leaders, and the organization which wished to reach this world as a public would have to speak in a hundred tongues to a hundred or so diverse interests.

Nevertheless, this is the public, as it was in the days when it consisted of the few and privileged, to whom it is most worthwhile for an organization or a business leader or the man of affairs to speak. For, also as it was in the old days, it is the group through whom ideas, values, concepts, and enterprises are given validity and acceptance by the rest of society.

How then are these leaders reached by an organization or by the man of affairs? What are their characteristics? What makes them leaders? What gives them their influence?

You as an opinion or taste leader

Sociologists and those interested for commercial reasons have during the last few years spent some time studying the so-called opinion and taste leader in our society. These studies were originally triggered by the finding that mass media do not work either as directly or as simply as had been supposed on the mass audience to which they are beamed; that, in fact, they have surprisingly little effect unless supplemented or reinforced by climate of opinion and personal influence.

These findings should not perhaps have been so surprising. People are influenced more by people, by the full power of the tangible personality, than by disembodied voices, or shadows on a screen, or printed words or screaming banners. They are influenced by those they admire or trust, by those who seem to them experts or authorities, by those whose disinterestedness they are sure of, and by the casual word, the aside, the tentative remark thrown away, far more than by the great, booming, pounding sea of advertising and blather, no matter how impressive or skillfully produced.

But these findings also revealed that in any community there were certain individuals whose opinions and tastes carried more weight than anyone else's. These people, it turned out, were not necessarily concentrated in the higher strata, the more educated classes, or the more impressive positions;

they were almost evenly distributed through every class and occupation. Furthermore, the same person was not usually an opinion or taste leader in more than one or two areas or on issues outside of his supposed competence. There were opinion leaders or taste leaders in politics, fashions, books, motion pictures, the buying of groceries, public affairs, décor, and so on; and, as might be suspected in an open society, the leader in one field might or might not know the leaders in the other fields, depending entirely on the nature of their interests and the accidents of location.

Nevertheless, it was found that all opinion and taste leaders shared three key characteristics which gave them their status and influence: (1) They were, as might be imagined, in sensitive positions which were regarded as giving them special competence in the field in which they influenced people. (2) They were unusually well informed; they read more, listened to the mass media more, were more sensitive to the tides of fashion and change; they knew more people, were more gregarious, and particularly, they communicated more. Finally, (3) they cared; they showed a much higher degree of real interest and warmth toward their subjects, were much more likely to have cherished opinions and to have developed cherished tastes; and they gave more of themselves to whatever they became interested in.

It is perhaps not too astonishing that these three qualities appeared in almost every case of an opinion or taste leader. They might well have been deduced from man's long experience with those who have influenced him most through the years, but it is comforting to know that the sociological findings fully support them as characteristics. It is also worth knowing that to reach the rest, it is important to reach first these leaders. How then can the man of affairs or the organization go about reaching them? Three possible approaches suggest themselves.

1. Identify those in any community, profession, trade, or industry who are considered the authorities in their fields.

These men are not usually too hard to find. First, "everybody knows them." Second, they have written, given talks, sat on panels, and appeared on forums on their subjects. Third, they are usually referred to as "the man who can help you out here."

2. Study their work, their activities, their personal backgrounds.

You learn best how to approach influential people by reading their work, talking with those who know them, and generally finding out their ideas on issues with which you hope to reach them.

In an organization, there is usually someone who through his interest and participation in the field in question can single out and approach the opinion leaders of that field. He can contact them knowledgeably with any concepts, material, or problems the organization may have relevant to their fields of interest.

One of the characteristics of opinion leaders, as already noted, is their extreme responsiveness. Their only problem is usually the matter of time. There are usually so many demands upon them that your claim upon their attention will have heavy competition.

3. Be sure the thinking and material emanating from the organization to them is of first quality.

The best way to claim their attention is to produce work of first quality. This is, of course, the best way to claim anybody's attention, but opinion and taste leaders are more sensitive to quality than the rest of us and respond more strongly to unusual quality. This is one of the elements which has made them leaders.

It is obvious that this ninth public, the Great World, in reality consists of an amalgam of the leaders of all the other publics we have discussed. From this great diversity of talent, which we call the Great World, experience seems to show that only one element of appeal can be isolated and that is quality; and, of course, quality or excellence is the most difficult of all the ingredients that can be built into a work or an enterprise and as rare as it is difficult. Nevertheless, this is the one secret of reaching all the publics we have discussed and perhaps the only truly important secret. All the other elements can be more easily and readily developed.

Of all the publics the organization needs to reach, however, this ninth public is the most influential, and of this public there is an elite to whom the business leader and the man of affairs might well, if he can, address himself. This elite was characterized by Schopenhauer as follows:

> No difference of rank, position or birth is so great as the gulf that separates the countless millions who use their heads only in the service of their bellies and those very few rare persons . . . who try to comprehend the wondrous and varied spectacle of the world. . . . These are the truly noble, the real noblesse of the world. . . .

Now we conclude this section on the nine publics of an organization. The division of those to whom an organization speaks into nine publics is, of course, purely artificial; and, as we have observed, these so-called publics overlap, but this concept has a certain usefulness in helping the organization consider how to reach all those who will have a bearing on its destiny. The publics suggest the kind of channels, forms, and media which may be most effective and the kind of message that would be relevant.

IV

PUTTING IT TOGETHER

Ingredients for a sound communications program

Speak with one voice. . . .

18

The sense of the whole: some ingredients for a sound communications program . . .

"THE SENSE OF THE WHOLE," CHESTER I. BARnard has said, "is the dominating basis for decision." In communications, the sense of the whole is vital to the effectiveness of an organization's messages and to the impression of integrity which an organization gives. As an organization, it should appear to be speaking and should in fact speak with one voice, and what one of its publics hears should not be contradicted or radically incompatible with what others of its publics hear.

This is not to say, of course, that every message to every public must be the same, only that the voice be the same voice in style and personality and the message at least conform to a sensible, overall, coherent company policy and objective. To secure this sort of compatibility and overall effectiveness, the business leader will need to know how to set up a coherent communications program to reach all the organization's publics, how to set up sensible lines of review and control of information flow, and what characteristics and requirements make for success in the operations of such programs. For, the fact is that communicating to a number of widely varying publics works best when planned and administered as an entity. There is best use of available resources, less duplication and wastage, and less confusion, and the organization's communications talents can be brought to bear on the most vital areas.

One important observation, however, needs to be

made at this point. We cannot understand organizational communications if it is to be regarded only as a management tool. An organization has a life of its own, and its communications needs go far beyond management's immediate purposes. If management does not provide the media to assuage "information hunger" or the talent to develop and sustain the channels and forms required for the organization's publics, the organization will, as we shall see in our considerations of some of the programs to be discussed, suffer in very vital and specific ways.

Nevertheless, in every organization, a rational overall communications policy and program can be set up, a program carefully constructed by management to help the organization reach its specific goals and still meet all of the other nonadministrative communications needs. Such a program would have four major requirements:

1. A climate for communications at the top. As the president of one big corporation remarked: "It is the chief executive who must first establish the right communications climate. It is he who should initiate and take an active part in the total communications program. It is he who must make clear that such an investment is not an on-again, off-again proposition—not a first-cut item when budgets get tight—not a process that can be assigned to staff people and then forgotten."

Nor is good communications to be confused with a good program of communications technology. We have used the term communications here primarily to denote the meaningful exchange among conscious beings based largely on language. While there has grown up a whole technology founded on the use of transmission devices, data processing, and retrieval systems, which has somewhat run away with the term communications itself, let us be quite clear. Only human beings can communicate in the full sense of the word, and no communication technology achieves communication except when a human being is involved.

To speak of a machine communicating with another machine, as is frequently done, is in the same category as speaking of a machine "thinking" as was suggested by such mechanists as Türing, whose proposed machine is famous in computer mythology. All these concepts are anthropomorphic, ascribing human traits to inanimate objects. Man's long love affair with the machine which has served him so well has led him to give it the same affectionate and fearful human or supernatural attributes as ancient tribes ascribed to natural objects such as trees and stones and sometimes animals. Thus, our legions of robots and Frankenstein's monsters parallel the golden idols and sacred trees of antiquity.

2. A policy that is spelled out in the following areas:

Why is there to be a communications policy? What is its essential purpose?

Who is to be involved in the program both in initiating (usually all of management) and in receiving (usually all of the organization's "publics")?

What is to be communicated? What types of information, knowledge, and material? What types are generally not to be communicated?

When is this information to be communicated? What is the timing on various types of material?

How is this data to be communicated? What media channels are to be used?

3. A practice which employs the skills and abilities of professional, editorial, journalistic, and other specialist talents to prepare, administer, and operate the program under the guidance of the policy as set forth by the chief executive.

4. A constant careful check on the quality of the communications content, material, and media.

To indicate some of the elements of an overall program, let us look at an approach requiring management participation, used by one of the leading organizations in its field, to see how such an overall communications program might be set up. Then we can look at three examples of actual programs for three kinds of organizations: a small, informal partnership, a medium-size corporation with two or more locations, and a large, international organization with many plants, branches, and subsidiaries.

A N OVERALL APPROACH

This overall communications approach involving management participation requires a certain philosophy and way of
looking at the organization which goes beyond its purely economic function. The philosophy runs something like this: An
organization like a man owes something to its community.
Quite aside from the economic assets of goodwill and profit-
ability, which are often offered as the only measures to be used
to justify the care and attention which an organization must
give to reach all of its publics constructively, the organization, if it is to meet its full obligations, must throw the weight
of its resources and influence in such a way that it adds its
best to the general good. Gaston Berger once wrote in another
context:

> The day before yesterday we followed unconsciously what
> was called Nature; yesterday we tried consciously to con-
> form to "nature," but today, our power having grown
> considerably, it behooves us sometimes to protect nature
> and sometimes to arrange it in ways which seem favor-
> able. . . . A reality is to be constructed and not events
> awaited.

In the same spirit, each organization would benefit from considering what its role should be and how it might best benefit
and influence the various worlds of which it is a part, and to
do this, it must ask its managers to step back from the press of
immediate daily tasks long enough to study and construct
what it and they have to say to the world. If the whole art of
management seems to consist, as some say, in the intelligent
and efficient allocation of scarce resources to the most effective, productive, and socially desirable goals, then the problem in communications becomes one of inventorying and assessing the resources and working out how best to allocate
them. Here is how this particular organization tried to do
this. It can serve as an illuminating pattern for all kinds of
organizations.

The chief executive set up a committee composed of himself and three of his major officers to survey their present

communications operations, to study who their publics were, and to consider how to reach those publics. The committee members opened their discussions by defining this program as a means to implement one of the organization's overall objectives which might be expressed as "the organization's obligation to reach and present itself effectively in those wider areas where its operations, products, and knowledge would prove useful and valuable."

The minutes of that committee meeting were unfortunately couched somewhat in the officialese so common even in policy instruments having to do with communicating, but a portion of those minutes, summarizing the sense of the discussion, will now be presented.

There were two major implications in this overall objective. First, it was stressed that it was not the organization's prime purpose—and indeed in most instances very little purpose would be served—in merely so to speak "getting the organization's name in the papers." The second and more important implication was that the organization was interested in reaching and presenting itself in these wider areas only if it had something useful and valuable to offer. This was a cardinal point of the objective, and *its full objective could be achieved, therefore, only by the true value to its various publics of what it had to offer.* This was not to be a program for publicity seekers.

It was suggested that a large part of the value of any program arising from these discussions would be in making this objective clear, indicating to each individual in broad terms what the company was prepared to do and presenting him with a general guide as to what he himself could do that would meet this objective and thus increase the organization's usefulness and enhance the organization's and his own stature within it.

In terms of the program under discussion, therefore—the company's communications program—these discussions were directed to (1) surveying what areas the organization should be reaching (2) determining whether it was reaching these areas and, if not, by what means it could reach them and (3) offering suggestions as to how to make the best use of available manpower and talent to implement these objectives and reach these areas.

What are we doing now?

Before going into these subjects, the discussion turned to the results of a survey, made under the committee's direction, of the company's present communications practices and participation.

A study of the results of this survey and certain analyses seemed to indicate:

1. that the organization's management was spending an enormous and disproportionate amount of time and effort in communicating with three of its eight relevant "publics"

2. that 60% of its communication efforts were concentrated in one field which had once been but was no longer its main field of profits

3. that little or no attention was being given to the organization's obligations in two very important civic areas

4. that the quality of its contributions varied quite considerably and in some instances was far below that which an organization noted for quality products should tolerate.

How should we reach our publics?

Publications. The committee now turned its attention to a study of the areas which the organization should be reaching. First, the publications it should be reaching with its material were discussed. They fell into four classes: (*a*) trade (*b*) general business (*c*) a few possible magazines of mass circulation and (*d*) books.

(a) Trade and industry publications

It was generally felt that the organization would do well to study the possibilities of developing subjects of value for a wider group of trade publications of a high quality and wide circulation in industries using its product (some 240 of the estimated 5,000 are listed in the Industrial Arts Index).

(b) General business publications

In this small group, it was felt the organization had material of interest and value which could be developed specifically for them.

One of the committee members cited the instance of a request from a famous magazine made to a member of top management for an article. Because of the pressure of work, the executive was not able to comply. The committee member asked the question: "Should not we consider such a request as a matter of top priority?" The consensus seemed to be that such requests should be accepted wherever possible. These publications were known to be extremely influential in top business and industry circles important to the company.

(c) Publications of mass or general circulation

It was suggested that there are from time to time subjects of general interest on which the organization has something valuable to say about its specific field and that it must attempt to prepare this material for general magazines.

(d) Books

The committee noted that at least seven book publishers had shown definite interest in whether members of management and the company's people had material in preparation for books. The committee agreed that these persons should be encouraged to complete books they have in mind if possible during their active careers rather than, as was generally the case, decide to put off such undertakings until they retire. The committee felt that books of interest and value to the technology and industry carry a heavy charge of prestige and can be important to the nation's and the industry's economy.

Audiences for speeches. The second section of the program dealt with the subject of audiences for speeches. These were discussed under two headings—industry and nonindustry audiences.

Industry audiences

The committee recognized that the organization had an obligation to participate fully, to do its full share and perhaps even more than its share in programs before all the relevant organizations in its industry. It felt that it might be useful to run a sample of the share of participation in relation to that of other similar large companies to see whether the management was doing its share, doing too little or too much. Around 25% of participation was considered fair, as high as 50% too much. The committee had the impression that management was doing a great amount of speaking before industry bodies and more than their share of serving on committees and that this was beneficial up to a point but that the quality of these talks could be substantially improved.

Non-industry audiences

In this area, the committee felt much studying must be done. The records showed that the organization's people spoke before seventeen different non-industry audiences, including management groups, chambers of commerce, civic groups, bank, insurance and other business groups and customer groups.

It was pointed out that there are in the U.S. today some 18,000 trade associations, of which about 3,000 are national in scope. Of these the organization's public relations group had selected as of probable importance from the company's viewpoint—115. In the three years studied, the company's men spoke at conventions or meetings of only a few of these. The question arose: to how many of these do the company and its people have something valuable or important to say and how can they reach these convention audiences to say it? The committee decided to study this list and consider how to reach the associations considered important as audiences.

A further suggestion was made that the company might develop seminars for groups of customers in various fields of experience.

Another question was that of whether to concentrate the organization's efforts on specific areas. It was thought that efforts in speaking and writing might well be concentrated in geographical areas where the organization was not receiving its share of the business and in those industries where its products were not being adequately employed, particularly in growth industries where there is a possibility of increasing the proportion of the contributions from that field. The electronics industry was named as such an industry.

The committee now turned to the problem of reaching the publics which the organization ought to be reaching. Four areas of discussion were suggested: (1) considering what makes material valuable to its various publics (2) assessing what the organization has to offer (3) preparing this material in a form suitable for these publics and (4) both letting them know this material is available and inducing them to want it and request it.

What makes material valuable

Three kinds of material were considered of value to the organization's publics (a) material which stimulated thinking in problem areas, crystallized and posed the problem often even before the problem became apparent to the public (b) material which solved problems and (c) material which educated, led to the exchange of views, summarized or synthesized information or helped raise standards in the industry and business world.

Preparing the material in a suitable form

Three approaches to the preparation of material for these publics were considered:

(a) In the realm of speeches before industry and technical organizations, it was considered that too often the talks had not been well enough prepared or had not presented anything of real value. Too often, representatives of the company had been placed on programs and not been able to contribute anything except a rehash of the same old subjects or merely ritualistic and pious sentiments that made no real contribution to the audience's evening. It was suggested that to gain the fullest value from talks here, members invited to speak should be aggressive in turning worthless or time-wasting subjects or material into those that have some value even, when necessary, by requesting and offering a different subject from the one assigned and in addition that every effort be made to *widen the reach of worthwhile material and increase the value to the audience by requesting, where possible, that the sponsor include other groups in the audience such as chambers of commerce or local businessmen who might be interested.*

(b) Secondly it was suggested that the various specialists in the company study the problems in their fields and develop articles and material for talks that are timely and of interest to people in business.

(c) And finally it was suggested that certain basic subjects with broad interests in the organization's general fields be developed and prepared in the form of full-dress articles or speeches. Possible subject areas might include . . . (and here 35 such subjects were named.)

Letting the publics know material is available

The problem of letting those who can use this material know that it is available the committee felt could be handled through public relations, etc.

Making best use of our scarcest asset

It was recognized at the outset that in carrying out this program, the organization would be making an expenditure of its scarcest asset—the time of its top management and major talents. To make the best use of this valuable commodity, therefore, the committee felt that research, writing and speaking efforts should be organized on a company-wide basis and at the same time additional assistance and talent from the outside might be used. The committee considered this problem of manning the program under four general headings:

1. Making the organization's people aware of the larger possibilities of material which is the product of their research or experience and organizing the material already available into a form that would cut down on manhours spent in preparation of speeches and articles on these recurring themes

2. Widening the participation in the general writing and speaking program by specific assignments and assign-

ing major executives to speaking engagements in relation to the value of the speaking engagement to the organization

3. Developing some evaluations of, and training in, speaking and writing efforts, and

4. Through fellowships or research grants enlisting the aid
of qualified men in educational institutions to make
studies and/or do research for the organization (and for
themselves) that will result in material of wide interest
to the industry.

Cutting down on manhours of preparation. Much valuable original material it was felt was "lost" because the possibilities of its use in article or speech form were not recognized. Some of this material, particularly that arising from
unusual work, could be preserved in the form of case studies
which might either be circulated through some of the company's internal publications or through research memoranda.

In addition, it was considered that certain basic material
on recurrent themes could be organized into either completed
articles or all-purpose formats for use by higher management
called upon for a speech or an article on the subject.

*Widening participation in writing and speaking ac-
tivities.* The question was raised as to whether the organization's communications activities were falling on too few
shoulders and whether there might not be a need to broaden
the base of participation. It was recognized that not everybody in the organization should be persuaded to enter upon
this type of activity, that managers must apportion their time
and activities in accordance with their desires and pro-
clivities and many do not make their best contributions to the
organization in this area.

However, it was considered that perhaps there should be
a campaign among management to spread the importance of
sharing this basic organization enterprise, particularly
among those who show interest and ability in writing and
speaking. It was suggested that officers might indicate to
their managers that their effectiveness in these activities
would be a part of the way in which they would be evaluated.

It was pointed out also that two people could sometimes be used in a joint authorship of an article, which spread the work and the recognition.

Improving present speaking abilities. The committee suggested four possibilities in evaluating and improving present speaking techniques: (a) instituting a speaking workshop on the management level in the present training program (b) encouraging toastmaster's clubs (c) securing the services of professors of speech (d) having an officer present at the first speech given by a new manager and encouraging and giving advice in a constructive manner. This, it was felt, would indicate that higher management consider this ability of value and importance and appreciate the manager's efforts in this area.

Assigning top officers to speaking engagements. Requests to speak are often addressed to members of management who are well known and who already have many more speaking and writing engagements than they can fill. The committee suggested that when such requests come in to officers who are already booked up, it might be wise to suggest, where possible, a substitute—either another officer or perhaps a man in the organization who has become an authority in his field. This would also help broaden the base of communication activities and bring less well known men to the attention of the organization's publics. The value of that speaking engagement to the firm should be a consideration in assigning an officer or expert.

Offering fellowships or research grants to instructors. Four kinds of outside help were considered in manning the program: (a) securing more staff assistance with writing and research abilities (b) finding ways of working out an alliance with professors as consultants (c) arranging a series of two-year fellowships with instructors who would act as research associates to the organization and perhaps spend their sabbatical or work part-time with the company, gaining practical experience which would be of value to them in their teaching and (d) making grants to instructors or others to make specific studies for use of problems of interest to the industry. It was suggested that perhaps these studies could be theses for the instructor's doctorate, thus being of great value to him in his own professional development as well as of value to the industry.

Formulating a plan

The session concluded on the note that when this program had been clearly enunciated and approved, it might be well to prepare for distribution a statement of the program and a statement of the individual's as well as the organization's contribution to making it work.

Value of total view

Through this summary, taken from selected minutes of that meeting, may be seen dimly the outlines of a truly comprehensive program. This kind of total view of an organization's communications is admittedly of broader proportions and requires greater management participation than many other enterprises would be willing to undertake. Nevertheless, the approach can provide a comprehensive and fruitful pattern for an organization's view of its management's and professional specialists' communications commitments. Now let us look at three actual communications programs in action: those of a small firm, a medium-size corporation with two or more locations, and a large, international organization with many plants, branches, and subsidiaries.

CREATING A COMMUNICATIONS PROGRAM FOR A SMALL, INFORMAL FIRM

A partnership of twenty partners and a staff of two hundred would not seem to require any special communications program. The firm described here is in a single location on one floor, and the members and staff see each other at least once a week. Nevertheless, this is the size at which some sort of formal communications program should be considered. The program will usually be simple and inexpensive, but it requires very specific planning and seven basic elements. It will be found useful for administrative purposes, for morale and motivation, and as a means of developing the firm's practice. The object of the program is threefold:

1. To keep partners and employees informed
2. To present the firm favorably to its clients
3. To present the firm favorably to potential clients, the business world, and, to some extent, the general public

The resources to be used are the partners' time, a staff employee's time, and a small initial budget of between $20,000 and $40,000. The program consists of the following elements:

1. A guide to policies, procedures, and practices of the firm and how they are to be communicated.

2. Establishment of a library of basic books and materials for the firm and for deposit of any speeches, articles, reports, or research papers by partners or staff.

3. Standardization of quality and style of all materials leaving the firm—letterheads, brochures, reports, etc.

4. Guides for and models of repetitive and important letters, major reports to clients, and other communications often used.

5. An internally reproduced weekly or biweekly newsletter of two to four pages on what is going on in or outside the office. This news publication would inform the staff of new business, and activities of members of the firm and staff, and bring to their attention items on which the partners would like their cooperation. Publication of this newsletter must be the duty of a talented partner or member of the staff, and sufficient time for its preparation must be allotted.

6. A well-designed brochure for orientation and recruiting purposes, telling about the firm and its practice.

7. A brief brochure or booklet to be sent outside the firm with helpful information about the field in which the

client offers its services. The services of the firm may be mentioned at the end, depending on the tone and modesty of the mention. The important element of this booklet would be its value to those in the firm's general field. It must contain information helpful enough so that it will be asked for by those the firm wishes to reach.

These represent the few sound, basic communications needed by a small informal organization. In addition, partners and staff might be encouraged to serve their profession or field in nonbusiness activities as well as in speaking before groups or writing articles for business or professional journals. Such efforts will build their reputation and that of their firm.

CREATING A COMMUNICATIONS PROGRAM FOR A MEDIUM-SIZE COMPANY WITH TWO OR MORE LOCATIONS

The fulfillment of the communications needs of the medium-size growing company is crucial to its continued growth and prosperity, and it is in companies of this size that communications facilities are usually found to be most chaotic and least adequate or effective. The reason seems to be that this area of the company's needs is not identified and is generally neglected by management, who confuse it with pure administration. Thus, communications simply grows like Topsy or does not grow at all, and the "information hunger" arising in such an organization has to be met at the informal, unorganized level where rumor, misinformation, and confusion are rife, and where no priorities can be established to distinguish between what is essential information and what is not.

It is surprising to find many companies of this size which have no plant or head-office papers by which to reach employees and keep them informed. Many such companies have comparatively large advertising budgets for reaching customers, but are unwilling to spend the much more modest sums necessary to reach other groups essential to their welfare, such as employees, shareholders, their suppliers, and even their own management. The important thing is to attack the problem as a whole, establish the climate for communications at the top, set up a communications policy, and then work out rationally the means for carrying it out. Here is a sound program for a medium-size company.

1. *Establishment of a written communications policy which outlines the philosophy, objectives, content, and means of communications with the company's various "publics."* This may often be better done with the assistance of a communications or public relations consultant, unless the chief executive has come up through communications. The consultant will make a study of the organization's communications needs, the kind of information sought; he will develop in cooperation with management a suitable program and reviewing system.

2. *Establishment of a communications or public relations department reporting generally to the chief executive to carry out the program.* The chief executive should always keep control of communications, for whoever controls communications sets the tone and "personality" of the entire organization. If the communications department reports to the personnel or any other staff or operating department, that department will set the tone and have a major influence on the "personality" of the company as a whole. Those who do not want to bother with communications do not want to bother with the "personality" of their organization.

3. *Securing suitable personnel and talent for the department to carry out the program.* This is the crucial area where many programs do not reach their potential. It must be obvious that, given an enlightened management and good content, the quality of the company's communications and the general tone of its printed material will depend almost entirely on the quality, skill, and talent of the professionals retained to execute them. It is useless for management to establish a good communications policy content and program and then have staff amateurs, no matter how good or loyal they may be, attempt to produce the necessary materials and instruments. The advertising group requires a highly skilled advertising agency to produce the company's advertising. The publications group in the same way requires highly skilled professionals, whether employed or on re-

tainer to produce its publications. Both require the freedom and the careful, intelligent supervision described earlier in connection with the use of the advertising agency.

4. *In a medium-size company, the communications or public relations department will usually have an advertising group and a publications group at headquarters* and perhaps a communications assistant, usually an editor-photographer, at each sizable location.

5. *The department's main operations will consist of:*

   — Operating established periodicals company-wide and at each major location

   — Producing other publications, such as recruiting brochures, staff handbooks, and annual reports

   — Overseeing and assisting the advertising agency with the company's advertising

   — Assisting in public relations work, such as publicity and handling of interviews

   — Developing all company insignia and printed materials, such as signs, letterheads, and intercompany memoranda

   — Assisting management and staff with reports, speeches, and other written instruments

   — Helping develop management and staff insofar as desired in writing and speaking skills

6. *Carrying out through appropriate communications means specific management efforts and objectives,* such as drives to increase safety, reduction of absenteeism, motivation to meet deadlines, reduction of defects in manufacturing, encouraging the purchasing of company products where appropriate, increasing loyalties and goodwill toward the company's goals, and encouraging self-development, education, and upgrading of skills.

7. *Satisfying the whole organization's "information hunger"* by maintaining suitable channels of the required quality to keep those interested in the organization abreast of new developments and informed of what is going on. The quality of this sort of communications will determine the quality of the personality and "social" envi-

ronment of the organization from which spring loyalty and the desire to excel.

Again, most companies of medium-size do not give the attention to this communications aspect of their enterprise which it deserves. Chaos and confusion in communications have a seriously damaging effect on the enterprise as a whole and in extreme cases may even threaten its survival. We now turn to a communications program developed to help save a large international corporation with many plants, branches, and subsidiaries which had met with severe reverses.

CREATING A COMMUNICATIONS PROGRAM FOR A LARGE, INTERNATIONAL CORPORATION

The situation described here may be used as a classic example of the crucial part communications can and does play in the life of a great, far-flung organization. This was a heavy-industry company which had suffered such severe reverses that the question of bankruptcy or dismemberment was no longer far fetched. A new president had just come in to meet this desperate situation. He found that he would have to reorganize the management structure and set up some sort of communications channels to get his new, vigorous policies and procedures through to his management, to workers in the various plants, and to the public.

The first necessity was to get over the fact that there was a new regime with a newly styled product, new policies, and new growth potential; and to do this, this president brought in an experienced communications director. What the communications director found was appalling. There were no channels of internal communications at all, except floods of memoranda, reports, and instruction notices emanating from various sources to various destinations without any real clearance or coordination.

At the plant level, information about the company, its management, and its objectives or occurrences at other plants or company locations was by grapevine or the public press, and often the company's own people were the last to be informed. Morale and confidence were low, and rumors were rife.

Time was of the essence. The communications director found that about two years earlier an outside organization had been brought in to study the company's communications setup (often the case) and that their findings had been gathering dust in some files (also often the case). The communications director pulled this report and studied it. He considered it sound enough and recent enough to base an early communications structure on without his having to resurvey the various plants and locations, at least for the present emergency. The structure he devised called for the following:

1. Standardized channels of communications to and from the executive, corporate, division, and plant levels

2. Content centered on corporate objectives

3. News given first to management and rank-and-file employees (as contrasted with their getting it from outside communications media)

4. Development of upward communications

5. Establishment of professionally designed and written and visual media.

The channels at the executive, corporate, and division levels were comparatively easy to set up: executive, corporate, and divisional newsletters designed for and keyed to the users. These contained the important information needed at each level, presented in a specific manner which would give its substance value, purpose, and the action to be taken clearly and briefly. This eliminated a vast flow of unorganized and verbose paper, and because executive letters came out every week and could be gotten out, when necessary, very quickly, sometimes in two or three hours, always within a day, and because they were crisply and accurately presented, they kept corporate and division executives informed effectively.

It was at the plant level that about two-thirds of the communications budget was allocated and that three-fourths of the new communications people were placed. The key to this structure was the communications coordinator, who was responsible for the coordination of *all* communications at the plant. These included:

1. Oral, written, and visual communications as well as communications counseling with other executives and departments

2. An upward communications program exemplified most notably in the Employee Suggestion program

3. A monthly newspaper and other periodic publications

The communications coordinator had one basic job: to make communications work and to do so by following established clearance procedures intended to safeguard against error or the blemishing of the company's reputation. When the new core of communications coordinators was assembled, the communications director set up a week-long conference in a location remote from telephones. During this week, the members of the group became acquainted with each other. More important, they reviewed their objectives and worked out the methods by which they would reach them. The week was a rigorous one and not all completed it successfully. One person was dropped from the program. The others were presented with certificates indicating their success. At the company headquarters, a staff function, Communications Services, was set up. Under this program was included the oral communications project in which staff people assist in preparing meetings, preparing flip charts, devising questionnaires to be distributed at meetings to test their effectiveness, and preparing posters and bulletins.

The results of the overall program were dramatic: a renewed confidence throughout the organization; prompt, accurate information; rumor swept away and replaced by clear, honest reports. A sense of belonging, of being part of a renewed enterprise sprang up as the company began climbing back to and even promised to surpass its old eminence. The program had one defect which we shall deal with later, but all in all it was a sound, effective job, and it helped turn the company around.

Large, far-flung corporations generally have rational, effective, and workable communications programs. They must in order to survive in today's competition. Where they sometimes fall down, and the defect mentioned in the case of our last example, is in the quality of the materials and forms representing them. If channels are adequate and seem to work well, there is no especial disposition to question the design and aesthetics of the materials and forms. The problem here, of course, is securing and retaining talent, and at times big organizations have a low tolerance for the striking or the unusual. What they desire and are satisfied with is simply the workable.

A second difficulty arises in the elaborate reviewing systems many big companies set up, which require a consensus in matters of taste; a consensus almost invariably means an inoffensive mediocrity. Thus, many fine designs and unusual or striking forms or media generated within large organizations have been watered down because members of management could not restrain themselves from imposing their less-developed and sometimes completely undeveloped tastes on the efforts of a creative person. They retained first-rate talent and imposed on it third-rate modifications.

The same is sometimes true in the editorial field, although here the mediocrity is generally, unfortunately, the editor's. But, of course, real talent is scarce, and professionals do the best they can. However, excellence in communications media and forms is highly desirable because the organization is often equated with its representative media as well as its products.

In the case of our third example, the dramatic improvements through good, sound communications over the chaos which obtained when the new president and his professional communications director took over largely obscured the fact that the aesthetic or artistic quality of the media and forms was low. The graphics were poor, the writing only adequate, the formats mediocre. No one cared in the beginning because management and the organization were so relieved to have some sort of communications channels that they soaked up the necessary information and materials coming through the pipelines like thirsty men in a desert oasis. Furthermore, the improvements over the former situation were so spectacular that any defects in quality of materials could not for the moment be perceived, but the effects of lack of artistic quality in the media will begin to show soon in the image which that company projects in comparison with its competition, and unless soon remedied this will present a major problem for the years ahead.

So, in setting up and operating communications programs, care in working out the objectives, in selecting the kind and quality of information to be transmitted, and in rationalizing the channels, media, and forms as well as careful attention to the quality or artistic or aesthetic value of the materials themselves are all of major importance. Lack of objectives makes it impossible to know what channels, media, and forms to develop, or of what variety and how extensive they should be to meet the needs of the organization.

Lack of care in selection of the information to be transmitted and in rationalization of the various channels, media, and forms leads either to chaos from an overflow of communications, the wrong kind of communications, or to an "information hunger" which may eventually lead to the organization's collapse. And lack of quality or artistic and aesthetic value in either the content or the materials of the organization's communications downgrades the "personality" and image of the organization and may make it unable to command the prestige necessary to meet its full objectives. Quality is becoming more important than ever before from an economic viewpoint in our highly complex and developing world.

So much for the characteristics and requirements of an overall communications program. Once more let us emphasize that every organization, whether large or small, should have such a cohesive overall program. Every organization should approach all those to whom it speaks as a unified whole with that sense of social responsibility and honor that its position in our society demands. It should have a carefully worked out, overall policy. It should in general have one policy, one voice. What it says to one public must be part of what it is saying to the society which it serves, and its management—the men who speak through it—must be skillful enough, knowledgeable enough, and honorable enough to see that this is so. The quality of our lives in this civilization will depend on these standards, this knowledge, and this honor.

Since all of us, whether we are conscious of it or not, all through our lives belong to organizations of various kinds—business, civic, or social groups; our community; our state; our country—a knowledge of organizational communications is useful and important, and the ability to develop a sound communications program can be of immense value. But the quality and substance of what we ourselves as individuals have to say to the world, the importance and value of what we are able to develop as a person to communicate, and our ability to learn what the future has to say to us are of even greater moment than any techniques or skills in organizational communications.

It is to this kind of communicating—the techniques of developing substance through the art of thought, of finding what it is our life-experience has to offer and how we can unlock it and bring it to light for the use of ourselves and others, and how we can give it the weight and originality that will project it into the future—in short, it is to the study of the development of substance that the final portion of this work is devoted.

V

RULING THE
MINDS OF MEN

The art of thought
. . . listening to the future

*There is always one moment when the door
opens and lets the future in. . . .*
GRAHAM GREENE

19

The art of thought . . .

IN THE YEAR 1665, TO ESCAPE THE PLAGUE AT Cambridge, a young man of twenty-four retired to a farm at Woolsthorp, where he had been born. From the age of fourteen, he had been occupying himself with mathematics when he should have been working on his mother's farm. He had finally been sent to school and then to Cambridge, where he matriculated at Trinity College. That year of 1665 and the summer of 1666 he spent in solitude, mulling over and reflecting on some of the problems of mathematics, optics, and force.

It was perhaps the most fertile single summer in the history of man's thought. For what this young man called "his poor and solitary endeavors," twenty years later culminated in a work of the human intellect that changed the world. It was entitled *Philosophiae Naturalis Principia Mathematica*. Newton's solitary summer reflections had made it impossible for men ever to see the world in the same way again. His *Principia* reshaped the universe.

In the winter of 1831, a young man of twenty-two, having failed in preparing for the medical profession at Edinburgh and taken a degree at Christ Church, Cambridge, tenth on the list of those who did not seek honors, boarded a ship bound for the Cape Verde Islands on a surveying expedition. For the next five years, he worked aboard this surveying boat, making geological and other observations, as it plied among the Galápagos Islands and visited Tahiti, New Zealand, Australia, Tasmania, Brazil, and on the way home, the de Verdes and Azores.

In 1837, he opened a notebook and began to collect in it some observations on the character of certain South American fossils and species of the Galápagos Archipelago. This voyage was enshrined forever as the voyage of H.M.S. "Beagle," and that notebook culminated, again more than twenty years later, in another epochal work of the mind, the title of which began with the words *On the Origin of Species* . . ., a title which still reverberates and a work which has again changed the viewpoints and concepts of men forever. Man has never been the same since Darwin took that fateful voyage.

Again, in 1885, a twenty-nine-year-old neurologist, having heard from a Viennese physician the story of an extraordinary experience in which symptoms of hysteria were cured by getting a patient to recollect under hypnosis the circumstances of their origin and to express the emotion accompanying them, went to Paris to study under the great J. M. Charcot and investigate hysteria from a psychological viewpoint. These psychological studies, however, met with immediate and vehement disapproval and resistance on the part of his colleagues.

Eight years later, he persuaded the Viennese physician Josef Breuer to collaborate with him on a book entitled *Studien über Histerie*, and the thirty-eight-year-old doctor took the decisive step of replacing hypnosis for retrieval of buried memories with a method called free association and suggested the existence of the unconscious mind and its powerful influence on conscious acts. For ten years, this indomitable man pursued his fantastic idea, working alone, demonstrating through case studies the workings of the unconscious and the various mechanisms of neurosis in a series of brilliant books that by the end of World War I had brought his discovery of the power of the unconscious to the world.

Once more, the thunderclap of an idea, worked into the structures of reality, had made the name of Freud a symbol of the exploration of the deeps of the mind and changed forever the course of human thought.

As a final example, in 1900, a twenty-one-year-old graduate of the Swiss Federal Polytechnic School in Zurich, having failed to find an academic position, took a job as a clerk in the patent office in Berne, where his main duty was the preliminary examination of patent applications. Four years earlier, when he had entered the polytechnic institute, he had not found the instruction very inspiring and had spent his time reading and mulling over the works of Boltzmann, Maxwell, Helmholtz, Hertz, and Juckhoff.

The patent office was a quiet place, and his job now left him ample time to contemplate the problems that really interested him. The result was four papers, which appeared in the year 1905. No invention ever submitted for patent in any patent office in the world would ever have the tremendous impact of those four papers. One created the theory of Brownian motion. One established the equivalence of mass and energy. One established the photon theory of light. One contained the special theory of relativity.

These were epochal enough, but in 1916, eleven years later, one of the most lofty and elegant edifices of thought ever constructed, the "General Theory of Relativity," was published, and the cosmos was shattered and remade. So the greatest work of the mind of man since Newton's had once more reshaped the universe, and Einstein, with his gentle and noble personality and towering intellect, became one of the great symbols of Man, the Thinker.

What is it, then, that enabled four men through, as Newton explained it, "the power of patient thought" to change the world forever, to change it more completely than could captains or kings, politics or governments, or wars? What can be learned from their labors? What ingredients and processes went into these massive achievements? And do these ingredients and processes have any applications to those of us of lesser gifts in smaller spheres?

"Genius can do readily what nobody else can do at all," Herbert Spencer wrote, and, of course, there is much truth in this. But these men themselves had some things to say of their accomplishments and the processes that led to them which have great relevance to our present inquiry. How do you find what it is you have to tell the world? And turning from the forms, the channels, the techniques, and the media for communicating as an individual through an organization, let us now consider what these men have to tell us, what it is that enables a man to unlock his life-experience and crystallize it into a form that can be used for himself and others and in behalf of his work.

*T*HE PROCESSES OF THOUGHT

"Genuine human accomplishments are always unconscious," Renoir said. The laws of thought certainly in part bear this out. Except in the most trivial and routine mental functions, no significant mental accomplishment, whether it be an important decision, a substantive information memorandum, a work of art, or a scientific discovery, can be effected without unlocking a man's unconscious to bring forth his life-experience to bear on the subject.

The main problem—and this is the main problem in bringing substance to any communication—is, then, the problem of bringing forth this life-experience. Much of what a man "knows" lies below the level of consciousness, and a surprising amount of that is lost because the techniques of retrieving it are never sufficiently developed to call this substance forth. Fortunately, something is known about how these processes of creation work and about the techniques which can be used to call forth and crystallize a man's life-experience in behalf of any specific problem or any work of the mind he may set for himself.

First, let us consider how the work of the business leader might differ from that of the leader in other fields and then consider in what way all creative work is the same.

The business leader or man of affairs is generally one who must make decisions based, usually, on very inadequate information and on hundreds of variables. He is under pressure primarily to act, not to think. His first job is to make a decision, and his second job is to make a good decision and to do this under pressure, and there is no use blinking the fact that this will be a large part of his "work" during a large part of his career. He cannot follow the suggestion in a John Barth novel, *The End of the Road*, as follows:

> Above all, don't let yourself get stuck between alternatives. . . . If the alternatives are side by side, choose the one on the left; if they are consecutive, choose the earlier. If neither of these applies, choose the alternative whose name begins with the earlier letter of the alphabet. These are the principles of Sinistrality, Antecedence and Alphabetical Priority.

If it were only that easy!

Another of his basic activities will, as he rises in his profession, be that of planning, of setting important, intelligent, and effective goals and working out the means of reaching them. In a changing, swift-moving world where products become obsolescent fast, new techniques and services are developed daily, and social values are reshaped or modified from year to year, this activity of setting goals and planning is never completed. It cannot be accomplished once and for all and then attention turned to execution and people. It is a constant activity which calls for all a man has to give it, including the years of his life-experience.

And finally, he deals with people, and the whole success of his enterprise depends largely on the talent he has to work with, that is, the people. True, some enterprises can survive with a sound commodity, routine talent, and a lot of good machines; but with most enterprises, it is the talent that makes the difference, not the commodity (which others can also offer) or the machines (which others can also offer) or the money (which can usually be obtained if one has the management talent). And the talent is what is most scarce and becoming scarcer. So the business leader works with men and must learn somehow to reach them.

How does he differ then from other leaders? Perhaps in a few ways: in his interest in business rather than in education or politics or art or science; in his need to make decisions under pressure, a necessity shared, of course, by political leaders; in his pragmatic concern for getting things done—less pronounced in scholars and research workers; in his complete dependence on people and their abilities and loyalties to achieve his objectives in contrast to the primary dependence of scientists and artists on their own talents for the achievement of their objectives. Einstein pointed this up when he said: "I am a horse for single harness, not cut out for tandem or teamwork; for well I know that in order to attain any definite goal, it is imperative that one person do the thinking and commanding." When one has said all this and not much more, one has said it all.

But the attributes and qualities which leaders must have in common are much greater. First, of all, of course, is energy. The leader's role in every field requires more vitality than does that of other men. It requires the surge of inner power, the ability to withstand heavy pressures, the ability to give of himself. Second, it requires in every field the ability to think, to foresee, to plan. And finally, there is the ability to reach others, either by the power of the personatity, of the style or of the idea. Here is where the laws of thought, the ability to unlock the life-experience and crystallize it in behalf of an idea, a plan, a goal, or a work of art, become of major importance. For men are reached by substance, by the ability to bring to bear this life-experience, and they are reached more deeply in this manner than in any other.

What then are the processes by which this power is developed? They are well known and there are four of them: the process of search and preparation, the process of incubation, the process of illumination, and the process of verification. These are the terms generally used by Helmholtz, the great German physicist, and by Graham Wallas in his essay on the art of thought. Let us consider each of them and how they operate.

Searching and preparing

The first and most painful part of the process of creating is the gathering of materials relevant to the subject and preparing them for use. If a businessman must make a key decision, he must first gather whatever relevant information he has on the matter and work out its implications. If an author is to prepare a book, he must gather the material for his enterprise, whether from libraries, special knowledge sources, his own notebooks, or the content of his own storehouse of emotion, knowledge, and memory, and he must mull over that material. The American painter Andrew Wyeth said: "All past experiences are endless in their return to me . . . The past gets richer and richer as I paint. At first, the picture is too thin but after six months I get to the bottom of realism." Even in such a work as a poem, there is the release of previously felt, stored, and worked-over memory and emotion. In remarking on a collection of his poems, Robert Frost once observed: "There are 300 pages in this book and they took me sixty years to write. I don't work by the day. I work by the year."

Of the search and preparation stage, the first part, the search and gathering aspect, is the easier. Many thinkers do not mind the labor of this part of the total process, and for the businessman who must make a major decision or devise a major plan, this function can be greatly eased and speeded up by having others do the routine part of gathering relevant facts and even processing some of them, as in setting up mathematical models through use of a computer. No one can really do for him the hard part of this stage, however; the weighing of material for relevant experience, the careful processing and evaluating. All of this must be done consciously first, before it can be turned over to the unconscious.

There is also a danger in allowing others to do certain parts of the search and gathering. In the case of novelists or historians and certain other artists, the search and gathering themselves are so important to the understanding of the material with all its implications and to the necessary plowing of the unconscious that this part of the work cannot be left to anyone else.

The preparation part of this stage, however, is the most difficult and painful of all. This requires the mulling over of the material, the considering of it, as Helmholtz said, "in all directions," working over it back and forth to try to extract the whole essence and import of it for your purposes. Every thinker at this stage suffers. For all is chaos; all is confusion. No patterns or coherence have emerged. No light in the darkness. The thinker is alone amid the mass of data, of terrifying unprocessed, uninterpreted material, heaped up to be probed, evaluated, studied, and reflected upon. He is left only to ask himself questions, for this self-questioning is at the heart of the process. It is no wonder that many at this stage skimp and turn aside. Few, except the unusually powerful and persistent, give the time and effort to preparation and to answering these questions that they deserve. There is the desperate desire to get it over with, to answer superficially or not answer at all, to convert this mass into something coherent and meaningful, and it is painful to have it all there before one, unanswered, resistant, and inchoate.

Here is the stage where lots of pencil work is needed, where questions must be formulated and discarded, where lots of experimenting with outlines or lists or implications must take place. There is a tremendous need to get it down on paper or canvas or sketch pad, or into figures or formulas—to get the material into your own work forms somehow. In business decisions, it might be the assigning of probability values to variables, or the weighing of costs, or the assigning of weights to various parts, or the trying to match men to vital situations—the mulling over of possibilities. This is the digging, the pencil work.

Next, and equally important, is what we have called "the plowing of the unconscious." There are a number of ways consciously to reach and stir up the unconscious, and according to the circumstances of his life and routine, each thinker must find the way which works best for him. Let us listen to creative men tell how they plow their unconscious. Here is Barrett Wendell, the scholar:

> My method of clearing my ideas is by no means the only one. I have known people who could do it best by talking; by putting somebody else in a comfortable chair and making him listen to their efforts to discover what they really think. I have known others who could really do best by sitting still and pondering in apparent idleness; others who could do best by walking alone in the open air; others by stating to themselves the problems they wish to solve, and then going about all manner of business, trusting from experience, to something they call unconscious cerebration. Each man, I take it, must find his own method; at different times each man may find different methods the best.

Here is David Ogilvy:

> The majority of businessmen are incapable of original thinking, because they are unable to escape from the tyranny of reason. Their imaginations are blocked. I am almost incapable of logical thought, but I have developed techniques for keeping open the telephone line to my unconscious, in case that disorderly repository has anything to tell me. I hear a great deal of music. I am on friendly terms with John Barleycorn. I take long hot baths. I garden. I go into retreat among the Amish. I watch birds. I go for long walks in the country. I take frequent vacations, so

that my b ain can lie fallow—no golf, no cocktail parties, no tennis, no bridge, no concentration, only a bicycle.

While thus employed in doing nothing, I receive a constant stream of telegrams from my unconscious, and these become the raw material for my creative work. But more is required: hard work, an open mind, and ungovernable curiosity . . .

Or here is how the great physicist Niels Bohr is described as plowing his unconscious. The description is from a biography by Barbara Cline:

Niels Bohr did not look intelligent. Also unlike Einstein, who possessed a flair for using words and expressed his thoughts easily, clearly and vividly, Bohr spoke tentatively and it was hard at times to make out his meaning. This was only partly due to the fact that his voice was soft and that he had a slight speech impediment. There was also the fact that he did not necessarily try to express his thoughts in the clearest possible way. For Bohr, words were tools: in doing physics he used words almost as much as he used mathematical symbols. Often when he talked he was not reporting a conclusion, but was working toward it as he spoke. Once one got to know Bohr and understand his way of using words, conversation with him could be exciting, especially if one questioned his ideas. In argument he was at his best.

These varied methods of what we have called "plowing the unconscious" require, however, conscious effort, and this whole painful stage of questioning, search, and preparation requires hard, unremitting work. This, of course, is the rub. As Graham Wallas has written:

There are thousands of "idle geniuses" who require to learn that, without a degree of industry in Preparation and Verification, of which many of them have no conception, no great intellectual work can be done, and that the habit of procrastination may be even more disastrous to a professional thinker than it is to a man of business.

In search and preparation finally, intensity is important. The amount of effort compressed into a measured time span, short enough to force attention and struggle and long enough to enable the thinker to gather and process a significant amount of material, is vital to penetration of the unconscious. The business leader, who must plan and make decisions, rarely has enough time to gather what he needs. He must make up for this by searching out and gathering the most he can within the limits of the time allotted him, for timing also is a key factor in his thinking.

To sum up, this stage of search and preparation calls forth a conscious, painful effort of self-questioning, of accumulating and handling a major volume of material, and of consciously attempting to stir up the unconscious. The South American author Jorge Luis Borges expressed it thus in one of his fine short pieces:

> He understood that modeling the incoherent and vertiginous matter of which dreams are composed was the most difficult task a man could undertake . . . much more difficult than weaving a rope of sand or coining the faceless sea.

So it is at this first stage.

The period of incubation

Now we move to the second essential element or process of thinking or creating—one just as essential as the stage of search and preparation but far less understood or heeded: the process called "incubation."

This process permits the unconscious to work on the problem or subject undisturbed, while the thinker turns his attention elsewhere. There are two key elements in this incubation process: the element of time and the element of distraction. In other words, the thinker after his intense struggle must put the problem or subject aside and do anything except think about it for a period of time. This is much more difficult to do than is generally realized. The thinker tends to continue to gnaw at the problem, to worry about it; and while he is doing so, the unconscious cannot complete its essential work for him. How then can he distract himself for the necessary interval?

Many thinkers have put aside their problem to go to bed and after a good night's sleep have awakened to find it solved or all but solved. Helmholtz tells how he would take long walks in the woods and how the ideas he sought would come to him unexpectedly then. "They have never come to me," he said, "when my mind was fatigued or when I was at my working table."

A. E. Housman tells how some of his finest poems came to him while he was shaving. Ogilvy indicated, as we have seen, many devices such as long, hot baths, gardening, listening to music, going into a retreat. Renoir told his son: "You should wander about and daydream a bit. It's when you are not doing much of anything that you are accomplishing most. Before you can have roaring fire, you've got to gather a good supply of firewood."

Graham Wallas in *The Art of Thought* summed it up as follows:

> Voluntary abstention from conscious thought on any particular problem may, itself, take two forms: the period of abstention may be spent either in conscious mental work on other problems, or in a relaxation from all conscious mental work. The first kind of Incubation economizes time, and is therefore often the better. We can often get more result in the same time by beginning several problems in succession, and voluntarily leaving them unfinished while we turn to others, than by finishing our work on each problem at one sitting. A well-known academic psychologist, for instance, who was also a preacher, told me that he found by experience that his Sunday sermon was much better if he posed the problem on Monday, than if he did so later in the week, although he might give the same number of hours of conscious work to it in each case.

How long must this period of incubation be? This, of course, depends on the length and intensity of the preparation and the magnitude of the problem or work. The unconscious might be compared in this art of thinking to a giant data processor, searching through the deeps of your life-experience to bring together all that is relevant to solve the problem or crystallize the subject. In a work of major proportion, such a process might require a slow intermittent series of illuminations over a period of years finally held together in one major flash and reduced to a written work—the eight years to formulate the theory of special relativity, the eleven to sublimate it into the major work of art, which is the theory of general relativity, or in the cases of Newton and Darwin the more-or-less twenty years of intermittent insights to pull the vast material together into the coherent master works the world knows. In small, less-complex work, a good sleep overnight may solve the problem, or a few hours of quiet distraction at a cinema or on some other activity which has nothing to do with the problem or work may be sufficient.

Work which has not been incubated remains inchoate and unfocused. It is still raw or partly raw material. Unfortunately, a large amount of raw material is foisted upon the world as unfinished work. Work that has not been ministered to by the unconscious will have no depth or insights (unless they are somebody else's). Thus, incubation is an essential process, a stage which must not be skipped if the work is to have any depth or coherence or be brought to completion. "For," as John Kenneth Gailbraith remarked, "it is with the creative man as with the cow, no browsing, no milk."

Eureka!

With the intense preparation and the period of incubation, the thinker now reaches the most pleasurable stage of his labors—the moment when his subconscious delivers to him the answer to the problem, the theme to the work which brings it all into focus. This is the well-known and delightful instant of illumination or, as it was called in the old days, inspiration. Its advent is often so pronounced and unexpected that it truly seems like a gift of God. It sends the recipient shouting "Eureka!" as it supposedly did Archimedes from his bath when the great mathematician realized the significance of displacement of a body in water, and it is truly one of the most moving, superb, and fulfilling of human experiences.

Poincaré tells how it came to him after the period of hard struggle and the stage we now know as incubation in his essay *Mathematical Creation:*

Disgusted with my failure, I went to spend a few days at the seaside and thought of something else. One morning, walking on the bluff, the idea came to me, with just the characteristic of brevity, suddenness and immediate certainty. . . . Most striking is this appearance of sudden illumination, a manifest sign of long, unconscious prior work.

But illumination may come at any time and under any circumstances, and it must be swiftly and immediately pinned down. Emerson has remarked on this:

Look after your thoughts. They come unlooked for, like a new bird seen on your trees, and, if you turn to your usual task, disappear; and you shall never find that perception again; never, I say—but perhaps years, ages, and I know not what events and worlds may lie between you and its return!

How then can the products of illumination be captured and preserved. The answer is, and has been in all literate times and ages, notebooks. Notebooks and journals are the secret of substance. How many great works have come from them. And no truly original work can be developed without them. They are and must become the repository of your illuminations, the brief ones as well as the important ones, the true as well as the false, for, as we shall see, there are false illuminations and many of them. But these products of that great Sargasso Sea of the unconscious contain the only originality the thinker will ever be able to develop, and this is true for the business leader, whose great plan or brilliant intuition or timing or unusual coup startles and edifies the business world, as well as the artist, the novelist, or the physicist.

Illumination is the third great stage in the art of thought and the most heart-warming. "It just came to me suddenly . . ." might symbolize the experience. And, of course, to the truly creative, this experience is frequent, exhilarating and nourishing. "In the case of a creative mind," Schiller said, "the intellect has withdrawn its watchers at the gate and the ideas rush in pell mell. Only then," Schiller concludes, "does the intellect review and inspect the multitude."

This is the common experience of the thinker. However,

for the single major work of thought, there must be the successive stages—all of them: search and preparation, incubation, and climaxing into illumination. Hans Zinsser has summed it up well:

> Even Archimedes' sudden inspiration in the bathtub; Newton's experience in the apple orchard; Descartes' geometrical discoveries in his bed; Kekule's vision of the closed carbon ring which came to him on top of a London bus; and Einstein's brilliant solution of the Michelson puzzle in the patent office in Berne, were not messages out of the blue. They were the final coordinations, by minds of genius, of innumerable accumulated facts and impressions which lesser men could grasp only in their uncorrelated isolation, but which—by them—were seen in entirety and integrated into general principles. . . .

"I can remember the very spot in the road," Darwin exclaimed years later, "when to my joy the solution occurred to me. . . ." This is the great moment, the moment of unalloyed delight, the moment of illumination. And now we must turn, leaving this profound and nourishing experience, to the last and once again painful stage: the stage of verification.

Is it really true?

The process called verification has many other names—in literary efforts, revision; in mathematics, proofing; in science, verifying through valid experimentation. It is the process which evaluates the quality of the ideas or works produced by the other three processes. It separates the true illuminations from the false, the valid work from the work that will not stand up, the dream and the illusion from the real.

Again it is a painful stage, particularly coming after the great stage of illumination. Every creative worker rises from his worktable convinced of the masterpiece, only to see it a day or two later abruptly shorn of its magnificence and lying there in all its mediocrity. The amateur always rushes out the work while it is still hot and the creative flush is upon him, only to be humiliated a week or so later to read in the cold light of day what he had sent forth into the world. The period of verification, revision, reassessment—call it what you will—is just as essential as any one of the other three processes, and the thinker must give it the attention and care and time it deserves.

Poincaré again describes this need for the cold look, the review:

> The need for the second period of conscious work, after the inspiration, is still easier to understand. It is necessary to put in shape the results of this inspiration, to deduce from them the immediate consequences, to arrange them, to word the demonstrations, but above all is verification necessary. I have spoken of the feeling of absolute certitude accompanying the inspiration; in the cases cited this feeling was no deceiver, nor is it usually. But do not think this a rule without exception; often this feeling deceives us without being any less vivid, and we only find it out when we seek to put on foot the demonstration. I have especially noticed this fact in regard to ideas coming to me in the morning or evening in bed while in a semi-hypnagogic state. . . .

What then is required in verification? Once again there are two elements: the need for time and quite possibly the need for conscious reworking, for illumination does not always present the work complete or in its proper form. There are some rare and happy few who need scarcely touch their work in revision. They are indeed rare and as fortunate as they are rare. Most thinkers find long hours of toil ahead of them after they have given the work that cold look.

And, of course, as indicated above, some of these products do not survive. Ernest Newman wrote in a preface on scientific thought:

> Science must adhere to the more direct activity of inquiry and experiment, adopting or discarding hypotheses without too much regard for consequences to philosophical systems or common sense. Philosophy may come after to repair the damage. Common sense must lick its wounds and recuperate as best it can.

This same ruthlessness must be a characteristic of the verification process. Not all consequences of an illumination may square with accepted patterns, and the author of a true work of illumination, when it stands up, must be prepared to protect it in the verification process, even if it goes against the established criteria for such work. John Maynard Keynes remarked about Newton: 'His experiments were, I suspect, a means not of discovering but always of verifying what he already knew.'' Verification then requires, first, time; second, the cold look; third, conscious reworking of material where necessary; fourth, destruction of that material which does not stand up; and, finally, protection of that which does. Darwin speaking of the crucial and significant essays of Wallace and himself noted: "Our joint productions excited very little attention, and the only published notice of them which I can remember was by Professor Haughton of Dublin, whose verdict was that all that was new in them was false, and what was true was old." And Newton, after the publication of his work on optics, bitterly regretted it for the storms it caused in scientific circles for many years afterward. True originality, of course, often shatters established concepts and is not usually apt to be received with either jubilation or equanimity. These are the hazards the thinker must face.

So the business leader and man of affairs who is to communicate anything of consequence must first find what it is he has to say, must subject the material he intends to present to the laws and processes of thought, and, as every leader who communicates in an organization knows, expect, if what he is presenting has any real originality or substance, that it will not be received with universal delight and approbation.

If, as has been widely suggested, communications should be dedicated only to the engineering of acceptance of the message, then those messages which by reason of substance and originality cannot be wholly accepted until their time has come must be ignored, and the pain and struggle of thought must be considered a waste of effort. It is one of the themes of this book that such is not the case, that, on the contrary, communication for its own sake is fruitless, and that there are enough trivial, easy-to-hear and useless communications in our world as it is. The earth is full of messages, of noise, and of a sea of voices, and how few are worth the hearer's attention! "There is no satisfactory substitute for brains," Edwin Stuart remarked somewhat unkindly; "but," he added, "silence does pretty well."

The truth is that no message of real consequence and substance can be developed without the partly painful, partly exhilarating processes of thought and creation described here, and that a valid message thus developed will be like the great idea whose time has come—irresistible. The problem eventually becomes not how to write or speak, or what to write or speak, or to whom, but how much you really have to say that is your own and that is worth the saying.

We have attempted to cover thus far the development of some of the techniques and skills of the art of communicating; to describe the levels at which communications takes place, the seven common business forms of communications, and the nine publics to whom those who direct organizations should speak. In this chapter, we have described the four processes of thought by which all important material for communications can and should be developed. We have pointed out that except for the simplest operational messages, works of the mind do not spring full blown for transmission. The content of the report, the article, the paper, the study, and the book does not present itself coherently or with substance. It must be developed through the creative processes described, and then it is ready for communicating.

Now, let us conclude by considering the other end of the communications complex, the listener; consider what the social scientists, the semanticists, and the communications intellectuals have to say about the theory and the mechanics of reaching him; and end with their thoughts on the future evolution of and prospects for communications itself.

20

Listening to the future . . .

"THE POWER OF ATTENTION IS THE MARK OF the cultivated man," Lord Chesterfield wrote. In our modern world, it is something more. It is a matter of survival.

In the midst of the noise, the clangor, the myriad voices, to whom is the business leader or the man of affairs to listen and how is he to get others to listen also, when it is important that they do?

These problems involve something more than the technique of listening, a talent which has also unfortunately been almost completely lost amid the distractions and pressures of the day. Everyone knows that today it has become harder and harder to bring oneself to listen and even more difficult to induce others to do so. From the dull instructor through whose classes the young man must sit to the beloved friend whose talent for saying nothing has inured his acquaintances to a bright but fraudulent show of attention, everything conspires to train a man not to listen out of self-defense.

This training continues as he moves into the business world or the world of organizations, where he is often forced on his way up to attend elderly bores and many who possess the deadly combination of superior position, inferior brains, and the compulsion to display both. As he continues his rise, however, the noise grows louder and the demands on his time and attention grow more insistent, and it is an unfortunate fact of life that the worth of what he does hear as he goes up appears to decrease in proportion as his own abilities and skills develop, while the requirement to listen diminishes as his own position improves.

He now reaches the heights of the business leader, and as a reward he must sit through endless and often useless conferences, dull dinner speeches, and long-winded, time-consuming ceremonies. He must watch the moving lips of colleagues whose words and thoughts he knows by heart. He must anticipate the lumbering observation, the incoherent explanation, the meaningless ritual phrases which are poured out over him day after day. He must observe the thousand courtesies due those with inferior ability or failing powers who have a more than ordinary claim on him. It is little wonder, then, that not only is the ability to listen lost, but the ability not to listen becomes highly developed.

It is little wonder, but it is dangerous, and the magnitude of the danger is in direct proportion to the importance of the successful man's position and to his power to affect the lives and influence the thinking of others.

It is not just that he has grown to prefer the sound of his own voice to that of any other. It is not only that the deference of others has begun to lend an exaggerated importance to his thoughts and words. It is not even that he may overlook the fact that he himself is fast becoming one of those eminent bores he so decried on the way up, men who do all the talking and none of the listening. In all of us, perhaps, these tendencies may be observed to increase with age and with the diminution of ability. It is that this loss of ability to hear, this positive skill at missing most of what is said and ignoring the world's distractions, may well shut off the man of affairs from the most vital listening ability of all—the ability to observe, sense, and apprehend change, the ability to hear the whisper of the future.

That mental rigor mortis which has set in, those value senses which have closed down, those lips which keep moving before one but from which no sound appears to issue, and those conversations that were missed are all warning signs. They portend a disaster which the business leader often cannot believe possible until it has actually happened. The ability to stand bores is, of course, important and useful, for bores often have something worthwhile to say, but the ability to keep open that sensitive inner ear which catches the voices of the future is a still greater and much more compelling requirement for survival for the man of affairs. It may mean the difference between the obsolescence of his organization or his ideas, or their usefulness and power in the world of tomorrow. It may mean his own usefulness and survival as a force for the future.

This, then, is the key problem, but before going more deeply into it, let us look at the two other important and useful functions of listening and inducing others to listen, abilities which appear almost to be becoming obsolete today and the loss of which may have serious consequences for the man of affairs.

The two abilities—that of listening and that of inducing others to listen—are bound up together. It can almost be stated as an axiom that one cannot usually successfully achieve the second without the first. If the man of affairs has lost the ability to listen himself or has developed to a high art the ability not to listen, he will find it increasingly difficult to get through to others and will often not realize when those to whom he is addressing himself are not on the same wavelength.

Let us consider first, then, some of the simple but vital rules in the art of listening to others; second, the problem of retaining others' attention; and go finally to the main problem of how to listen for the future, how to become aware of the nature and trends of what is being transmitted by the great communications media of our times, and how to keep abreast of the changing content of our culture.

*T*HE POWER OF ATTENTION ...

The art of listening to others is a simple one and well known. It is also an elegant one well worth cultivating, not only for its importance and usefulness, but also for the increased depth it lends to your thinking and the graciousness it adds to all business and social occasions. The man who actually listens and pays attention to what others are saying generally stands out like a beacon of courtesy and fine manners in a sea of what appear to be compulsive talkers. In business affairs, the listener is often sought after for advice even when he may have no advice to give, because the habit of listening he has developed enables others in his presence to order and clarify their thoughts. The man of affairs can have no more engaging and fruitful characteristic nor one more likely to bring out for him the best others have to give.

Before we list the seven simple rules offered to help achieve this kind of listening habit, let us note that this ability to listen is a part of good manners. The man who hears without appearing to listen or sits likes a clod, enigmatic and passive, while the person who is trying to reach him struggles to penetrate the façade, is not a good listener and must be placed almost in the same category as the man who pretends to listen but hears nothing. He is not a good listener because he has not made it easy or enjoyable for those talking to him to express themselves. The good listener has the faculty of drawing out the best a man has to give, of creating an atmosphere in which what is said seems to sparkle, and the speaker feels he is for some reason unusually eloquent.

This atmosphere has nothing to do with whether the listener agrees with what is said or not, or with his evaluation of the speaker. But if the busy executive does agree to give his time, and of course this is any man's most valuable commodity, let him give the time he spends listening with the same grace and flair as he does that spent talking.

With this in mind, here are seven suggestions which may help improve listening habits.

Establish an agreeable atmosphere

This means trying to put the speaker at ease. It requires in some cases that the talk be held where the speaker might feel most at home. In any case, it requires an easy, relaxed manner, a show of interest both in the speaker and the subject, and the avoidance of an impression of haste and pressure.

The business executive who turns every conversation into a timed contest, an inquisition, or a hand-to-hand combat, who seats the man who has come to talk to him across from a massive desk in a cold office with the light of the window in the speaker's eyes, is not likely to get the most from that speaker. The man who will get the most from listening, no matter how busy or pressed for time he may be, always gives the speaker that sense of leisure and thoughtfulness, and this impression is quite often a major characteristic of extremely busy, successful men. They appear to take their leisure, but everything gets done. Of one of the great men of affairs of our time, an admiring colleague once commented: "He always seems to have all the time in the world, and yet I know his day is scheduled from dawn to midnight!" It is the atmosphere, not the number of minutes that can be allotted, and the good listener is able immediately to establish this atmosphere, so that the speaker can say what he has to say freely.

Be prepared to hear the other person through on his own terms

One of the characteristics of the poor listener is his inability to listen to anything unless presented in a certain manner or in a certain tone of voice. Many of the messages most worth listening to are not always presented well or presented in an agreeable tone of voice. Sometimes the speaker through nervousness or misplaced emotions begins what he has to say either belligerently or defensively and, of course, in many cases boringly. The good listener makes sure that his own response puts the speaker at ease and seems to assure him that he will be listened to with interest and on his own terms. This kind of response usually establishes a rapport and permits the speaker to get to his subject more quickly, more dispassionately, and with better regard for its value and relevance to the listener.

Be prepared on the subject to be discussed

It is surprising how many men of affairs and business executives fail to take the time to look even in the briefest, sketchiest way into the background of a new subject that is to be brought to their attention. Obviously, if it is a casual conversation which sprang up on the spur of the moment on a subject with which the listener is unfamiliar, there is not much he can do about it, but most business leaders who allot their time to others have some intimation as to what the subject is to be and can at the least quickly consult someone else on it, glance at a recent article on it, or otherwise brief themselves in a minimum amount of time. This will make them much better listeners, will enable them to evaluate much more quickly and intelligently the speaker and his subject, and will increase both the worth and the amount of what they get out of the conversation.

Evaluate the speaker and make allowances for his circumstances

Most of us make a quick evaluation of any speaker to get a rough fix on how much of what he will say can reasonably be expected to be either relevant or valuable. While this is only common sense, the good listener has a much higher tolerance than a bad listener and will try not to prejudge too sharply but, insofar as possible, to get what is being said rather than who is saying it.

He will also take into account the circumstances. A man who has forgotten his notes before he comes to talk over a project or is under severe strain is not necessarily to be judged by the disastrous situation he finds himself in, nor is the content of what he says. Yet many business leaders, as they get older and hardening of the prejudices sets in, will miss the value of what is said because the speaker spoke under difficulties or even because the tie he wore was of an unsuitable color. No listening impediment is more common or more disastrous than the neurotic prejudging of a man because of his personality or circumstances. Make allowances and then listen.

Avoid getting mentally sidetracked when subjects are not central to the issue or touch on sore points

A good listener takes the valuable parts and holds those aspects which arouse emotion in him in abeyance. He does not, however, avoid listening to those aspects of the subject with which he does not agree or which are sore points with him. A poor listener often mentally edits out remarks he does not like or will unconsciously distort meanings to avoid having to come to grips with a viewpoint he resents. The good listener is tough minded. He hears it as it is, not as he wishes it were.

Second, he does not daydream while someone is speaking to him. The mind moves much faster than the tongue, and the intelligent man completes thoughts with much greater speed than the speaker can speak them. He, therefore, will use the time constructively either in considering the merits of the thought or in examining its implications. He must, however, be there when the next thought begins lumbering through. Interest is what holds the mind on the track, and interest, the ability to place oneself in a subject, will insure that little is missed.

Listen for and summarize basic ideas

No device is better for grasping what is being said than that of attempting to summarize mentally the main points. This quickly becomes a habit and does wonders in pointing up both the strong ideas of a subject and those which may need clarifying.

Sometimes, if the summary indicates a particularly muddy area, the listener will do well to ask the speaker gently if he would clarify the point before going on. Such interruptions, if not too frequent, rarely put the speaker off and, on the contrary, may help him to clarify for himself what he is saying. They will also indicate the listener's warm interest.

Restate the substance of what you have heard to the speaker

This technique for clarifying and pinning down the substance and meaning of what is said is perhaps the most effective of all the techniques for the listener. More mistakes and misunderstandings have been avoided by this habit of restating what was heard than by any other oral device. It also fastens the substance of the discourse in the listener's mind so that he remembers it better, and finally it tends to bring out the real import of the discourse so that the speaker himself sees the implications of what he has said. All in all, the listener will find this a very useful and effective habit to develop.

*I*NDUCING OTHERS TO LISTEN TO YOU

One of the great discoveries of recent years is that nobody listens. A further discovery has been that when people do by some miracle listen, they only hear what they want to hear. And a third major and initially stunning discovery has been that a great proportion of what has been thought of as communications is not communications at all in the sense in which we are using the word; it is either self-expression or ceremony. You will, of course, be struck by the remarkable fidelity of these findings and most others on communicating to what we all know of human nature, and you may conclude that human nature militates against rational relationships. How, then, you may ask, can we best induce others to listen to us, either as individuals or as a group? How can we be effective in personal communications and in reaching large numbers?

There has been a great deal of research in this area in recent years—research and experiments by psychologists, social psychologists, sociologists, and political scientists; experiments associated with the names of Paul Lazarsfeld, Kurt Lewin, Harold Lasswell, Walter Hovland, and their followers and associates, and a brief summary of some of their findings may be enlightening. These findings may be summarized under three headings: understanding the main ingredients of the communications process, getting over meanings, and the theory of persuasion.

Briefly, the communications process has three main elements: the sender, the message, and the receiver; and the man of affairs should know something of what has been discovered about the role of each in getting people to listen.

First of all, the role of the sender or source, as might be suspected, plays a large part in the credibility or validity of any message, and this has certain implications for the man speaking to others.

Obviously, it is difficult for a person to look objectively at himself as the source or sender in the three-element communications formula. For to himself as a source, he appears to have complete credibility. He may sometimes doubt the capacity or intelligence of the receiver or even worry about the technique of transmission or the form of the message, but of himself as the source he rarely has the faintest qualms.

It was Churchill who remarked that in a speech what matters most is who you are, then how you say it, and finally what you say. Alas, to those who have had to listen to eminent bores (not Sir Winston), this has seemed all too true—and usually to the detriment of communications itself. But his thought states a general principle of human nature, and the man of affairs who wishes to get others to listen to him must first examine himself as the source and see how he as the sender will affect the meaning and the impact of the message. In practical terms, it is sometimes better to have one's message reach certain listeners as emanating from another source than oneself, and every man of affairs has had the experience of having to decide who should be the one to make an announcement or to present a project.

In casual conversation, in the issuing of orders, and in the making of policy, the nature of the source has often ludicrously distorted the intent and effect of the message. The president of a big company wonders idly whether it might be a good idea to leave off the company seal on his note paper. He is shocked to find a few days later that all the company seals have disappeared, including those on newly manufactured products. The executive vice president remarks casually that he does not care too much for one particular photograph in an ad, and abruptly the message arrives at the advertising agency: "No photographs in our ads from now on." In the other direction, many a man of affairs is equally shocked when, say, in a talk to a group of labor officials, one of his most valid ideas is bitterly decried, and the next day he finds it being enthusiastically applauded when suggested by one of labor's own leaders.

Yet it is surprising how naive many leaders have been about the influence of themselves and their backgrounds in getting a response from a listener.

The second aspect of the influence of the source in getting a message accepted is the need to examine one's own prejudices and emotional set, for there are certain kinds of messages which have no validity when emanating from certain sources. The message which is blatantly self-serving, for example, rarely has much credibility, and the leader whose background includes elements which might prejudice the message must study how these elements might be so presented that they can be turned around from liabilities to assets in validating the message.

These are examples of the kind of findings on the sender. Let us now look at the findings on the message and the receiver.

Getting over meanings

The problem of meaning is an old and apparently insoluble one. Semanticists have devised endless delightful puzzles which show how easily people confuse value judgments, assumptions, and inferences with facts, how simply meaning is distorted by change of context, and how careless people are in the ways in which they alter meanings to conform with desires or whims or subjective needs. An example is demonstrated in the engaging experiments of Professor Festinger to show what he calls "cognitive dissonance," a common situation in which a person will change his opinion or exaggerate a statement to relieve the strain of having behaved in a way not consistent with his earlier opinions or beliefs. Since we are all in the same boat, however, in all of these human failings, we may look with sympathy at the problem of getting meaning over to others. Again, the wonder is not that slips in meaning occur between the sender and the receiver but how much of meaning does get through and how fully we are able to reach each other.

The Bible has a phrase, "He fashioneth their hearts alike," and this, of course, expresses well the simple basis for our ability to reach others. There is "a common market in meaning" which lies in the fact that all of us share basic biological, emotional, and purposive responses as well as the common traditions of our culture; and, in most cases, we need only look into ourselves to understand others.

Nevertheless, much can be learned by isolating and looking at the three elements of communications mentioned; and, in getting over meanings, some of the findings on that element called the message are of interest. Let us list them:

1. Difference in background, experience, and temperament between sender and receiver cause usually slight, although in some cases great, differences in meaning of a message as between one and the other. The words "democracy" or "freedom," for example, vary widely in meaning from one culture to another.

2. Messages like words have a denotative, that is, a dictionary or literal meaning, and a connotative or overtone meaning. A steak may have the denotation of a segment of a burnt, dead cow, but its connotation makes it attractive and palatable while the denotation does not. The words will not convey the right meaning without the right tone.

3. Messages have latent as well as literal meanings. The tone of voice may change the meaning completely. Consider sarcasm and irony. Most messages have a significant, though usually easily grasped, load of latent meaning.

4. Messages have different meanings in contexts.

5. Messages to be acceptable must conform to or be tested against group norms or values. One group's meat may be another group's poison. Unpopular ideas (that is, ideas not acceptable to one's peers or reference group) are harder to put over. They must be somehow channeled or partly channeled into the accepted framework.

6. Meaning is often the slave of subconscious and emotional needs. What a man says may not be what he means. He may complain constantly about the job. What he may mean is: "I am not getting along at home."

While these findings may seem somewhat commonplace and perhaps too well known to merit the amount of attention given them here, they have certain implications which can help the man of affairs understand something about the art of persuasion. Let us now look at some of these implications.

How can people be persuaded?

We shall now try to answer seven key questions about the art of persuasion. These answers are based on some of the findings of the psychologists and social scientists referred to above. The questions are as follows: (1) Can people be persuaded? (2) If so, who can be persuaded? (3) How can people be changed? (4) What appeals are most effective? (5) How are ideas put over? (6) How are mass audiences reached? (7) What have been found to be the effects of mass communications?

Let us begin with a fundamental question which strikes at the heart of our assumptions. Can people be persuaded?

The answer is a qualified yes, depending on the person and what he is to be persuaded of. Human beings have a surprising range and variety of tastes and interests and are by far the most adaptable of living creatures. However, it may come as a surprise to many that, despite our modern folklore, people are not robots. They cannot be manipulated, turned on, plugged in, indiscriminately told what to do, or programmed by any simple psychological devices.

They are varied and complex. They carry within them not only the billion impressions of their environment but the thousands of hours of life they have lived. Even a twenty-two-year-old has lived some 190,000 hours of life, which cannot be manipulated by an hour or so of television or by a business propaganda campaign but which could be and have been changed or sweetened by one moment of the exact, right line in a book, or the scent of autumn leaves, or a smile, or a beautiful day at the exact right instant of his life.

Thus when we speak of persuading, we assume limits and a tentativeness about the results which must be kept in mind.

Who can be persuaded? as is well known, some people are easier to persuade than others. Social psychologists, such as Hovland, Kelly, and Janis, have made studies of the kinds of people who are most persuadable by temperament and those who are least. Briefly, the findings are as follows:

Highly persuadable: men with imagination, who "respond with rich imagery and strong empathy." Sensitivity and intelligence are apt to make a man open to alien ideas.

Highly persuadable but so easily influenced that their opinions can be easily counterswayed: men with low self-esteem, typical indicators of which may be shyness, lack of social poise and self-confidence, and passivity. Also, "other directed" men who secure their values largely from their peer group and are thus usually quickly influenced by changes in opinion or in fashion.

Resistant to persuasion: dull or hostile personalities. The extreme form of resistance to persuasion is, of course, the paranoid type. Highly aggressive personalities and those who lack normal responsiveness remain relatively uninfluenced by any form of persuasion.

How can people be changed? The experiments on how people's opinions can be changed have centered largely around three kinds of studies: the order of the presentation, the effectiveness of source, and the effectiveness of fear-arousal as an appeal. Briefly, the findings as summarized by Schramm, Maccoby, McGuire, Rosenberg, and others, are:

1. For those already of an opinion, presenting only one side, the favorable, is the more effective. For those opposed, the two-sided communication is better, that is, presenting both sides of the question.

2. While no difference was observed in the proportion of people who changed their minds in the direction originally advocated, whether given a one-sided or a two-sided communication, those given the two-sided communication, the opposite side first, proved to be highly resistant to the effects of a subsequent effort to change their opinion again to the contrary viewpoint, while those given only one side were not. Apparently, presenting the other side first has a certain immunizing effect against counterarguments.

3. When contradictory information is presented by one person, material presented first tends to be more credible than communications presented subsequently, but interposing some time-filling activity between the two presentations can eliminate this primary effect.

4. The influence of order of presentation is weaker on persons who are more than usually interested in the subject.

5. Placing first the communication whose contents are

highly desirable to the people involved is more effective persuasion than is the reverse order.

6. When presenting arguments contrary to the position advocated, the communicator should give his own side first rather than second.

7. With regard to the influence of authority, it was found that while the prestige of the source is important in the persuasiveness of a message, this difference appears to dissipate over a period of time, and the message must then stand on its own. In these experiments, four weeks after the message was given, the content remained, but the source, whether prestigious or not, was apparently forgotten, only the content retaining its influence.

What appeals are most effective? Turning from the findings centered around order of presentation and the influence of authority or source, let us consider some of the findings having to do with appeal. It is well established in our folklore that people are primarily swayed by their emotions, and that if one can gain control of their attention through emotion, one can persuade. That this is just as unrealistic as the opposite supposition, namely, that people are wholly rational, is easily borne out by practically all the experiments so far made in this field. The man of affairs will have found through experience that generally people are rational and well aware of their own interests, that they are not to be swayed by senseless desires or passing emotions on matters of any import, and generally that such appeals are more likely to be distrusted than otherwise. Even such a powerful emotion as fear when used on children produces surprising results, as shown in the following experiments.

In using fear as an inducement with children, the experiments of Janis and Feshbach appear to show surprisingly that high fear-arousing appeals are less effective than more moderate or minimal fear-arousing messages. The minimal fear-arousing presentation (in this case on the consequences of not brushing teeth) proved the most effective, while the high fear-arousal appeal—pain from toothaches, afflictions such as cancer, paralysis and blindness resulting from extreme cases of bad teeth infection, etc.—was almost completely ineffective. Apparently, the high fear quotient arouses strong defenses. Similar experiments on adults made on the dangers of the atomic bomb had the same results.

This is not to say, of course, as any salesman can tell you, that emotion does not have a persuasive effect, all other things being equal. Nor that sentiment cannot carry great force when properly used. Robert N. McMurry concludes a delightful article in the *Harvard Business Review* on the mystique of supersalesmanship with these paragraphs:

> Typical of such a sales force's enthusiasm is the close used with great success by one specialty salesman of silverware. With his samples he carries two tall candlesticks. As he approaches his close he places his gleaming silver place setting on black velvet display pads on the dining room table, lights his candles and turns out the lights. In the romantic atmosphere which he has thus created, he makes his final pitch. He tells the prospective housewife:
>
> "Madame, there are three apocalyptic moments in every woman's life: when the man she loves tells her he loves her and wants to marry her; when she holds her firstborn in her arms; and finally when she looks down on her first sterling silver table service. Sign here, Madame. Please use this pencil and press hard; there are four carbons."

The kind of appeal, the kind of persuasion which lasts, however, and the appeals which make their mark on important issues lie deeper than emotion or sentimentality. While the carnival barker still draws them in and the confidence man still makes his quick killing, the man who would change the thoughts and lives of others must operate at a profounder level and offer a far better quality product; first, his own sincerity and depth, second, his own substantial thought and deeply felt desire, and, finally, what is true and what will stand up without him.

How are ideas put over? our next group of findings, that of understanding the ways in which ideas and innovations are gotten across, is associated with the work of a number of sociologists and social psychologists such as Lazarsfeld, Berelson, Gaudet, Dodd, and many others, who investigated the role of opinion leaders. Their findings are well summarized by Dr. Elihu Katz in an article on the diffusion of new ideas and practices. Dr. Katz lists six conclusions reached from a number of famous experiments:

1. The influence of other people on specific decisions tends to be more frequent and certainly more effective than the influence of the media. This was shown in a study of voter influence in the 1940 elections, in which it was found that, first, very few people changed their voting intentions during the campaign; secondly, among those few who did, the major source of influence was not the great mass media—radio speeches, newspaper editorials and so on—but other people: family, friends, co-workers.

2. Those who influenced others tended to be persons close to the people whom they influenced and tended to share the same social status. It was almost as rare to find someone of higher social status directly influencing someone of lower status as vice versa.

3. Close associates tended to hold opinions and attitudes in common and were reluctant to depart from the group consensus even where a mass appeal seemed attractive.

4. As indicated earlier, group leaders tended to specialize in the type of leadership they exerted. One would be an influence in fashion, say; another in marketing, etc.

5. Influence tended to flow from the more sensitive and aware to the less sensitive and aware until it was halted by the imperviousness of those who were completely resistent to change.

6. Those who diffused ideas—opinion leaders—were more exposed to media of all types than their followers, particularly in their own spheres of interest.

These studies appeared to show that a pattern was followed in the diffusion of an idea or an innovation. The pattern showed three stages: (1) the idea is presented or the innovation tried out by a small number of "advanced" or cosmopolitan persons, who have picked up the idea or innovation in their reading and listening and who, having tried the idea or innovation out, pass it on to their friends and followers; (2) in the second stage, it spreads fast because of obvious advantages and the tides of fashion; and (3) in the last stage, it becomes the norm, and the older, more isolated members of the group reluctantly take it up.

One basic and paramount principle seemed to hold in putting over any new idea: not only must it be accepted by the opinion leaders, but it must fit into the framework of the culture, and if it is a real innovation, it must somehow be channeled into the prevailing value system of the society. All ideas or changes to secure acceptance must somehow be made compatible with the prevailing patterns of ideas and, in order to conform, must often be initially modified.

How are the mass audiences reached? Again, the findings of sociologists seem to indicate that mass communications do not reach mass audiences in the simple, direct manner that common sense might suppose. Mass media depend for their effects upon a complex network of specialized personal and social influences. Furthermore, they compete, no matter how intense and powerful they may be, with a great many other more profound influences: education, family life, work, personal interests, human goals and needs. Thus, it would seem that, except where institutions have almost completely broken down as in revolution, war, or social catastrophe of one sort or another, and the individual has as a result been deprived of any group support, thus being turned into part of that horrifying phenomenon, the mob, there is no such thing as a mass audience in the simplistic sense. There is the mindless mob where all intelligence and control have been suspended, and there is the individual who hears the products of mass communications in exactly the way he wishes to hear them and who in general takes the message from them that he wants to take.

These individuals can be reached, then, only through their opinion leaders and in the context of their own culture and lives. They cannot be overwhelmed by either the volume or the skill of the mass media alone. What, then, have been found to be the effects of the mass media we hear so much about?

What has been the effect of mass communications? We can conclude our inquiries into the subject of persuasion with this final question on the subject of mass communications. What influence does it actually have? Is it really the modern Frankenstein's monster that social critics say it is? Have its junk programs debased our culture? Have the dramas of violence and disaster which have constituted the main fair of television led to increased crime and a taste for murder? Have the constant din and furor destroyed the leisure and ability to contemplate, to think, and to create?

Or on another level, are the mass media binding the earth's peoples together; planing down the differences among men; standardizing tastes; increasing a similarity of viewpoint, values, and desires; and gradually converting the world into a single culture?

Before considering the second set of questions, let us see what social scientists have to tell us about the first. What influence does mass communications actually have in persuasion? The social scientists have some interesting answers, and they bear out what has been found to be true of all kinds of communication.

First of all, people tend to listen only to opinions that agree with their own. This the social scientists term "selective exposure," and it renders a great deal of mass communications as well as other communications ineffective in changing opinion. Selective exposure applies also to tastes, forms of entertainment, and culture. One listens generally to programs which one has learned to like and avoids others. Thus, it is useless to urge a station to play only good music and so upgrade taste. Those who like good music already will listen; those who have not learned to like it will not. In political discussion, the viewer generally listens to and looks at his own candidate and tunes out others.

Second, if he must consider a point of view contradictory

to his own, he will tend to misread it or to conform it more nearly to his own preconception. This is selective interpretation. One interprets messages the way one wants to hear them.

Finally, people remember material which supports their viewpoint and tend to forget that which does not or opposes their viewpoint. So, memory is also selective, and mass media must run the triple gauntlet of this selective process in exposure, interpretation, and ability to remember. Thus, despite its great power and pervasiveness, mass communications is not much more effective in changing behavior or persuading than any other form of communications, and in many cases is much less effective than interpersonal communications.

What mass communications does do, however, is to offer the viewer or listener much more of what he wishes to hear, thus tending to reinforce his existing opinions and tastes, and this reinforcement aspect, sociologists seem to feel, has been its principal effect.

Does this mean, then, that mass media can have no influence? Of course not. There are times when people are ready for change. At such times, they listen and may well be influenced. Mass media may have great influence where no opinion or taste has been formed as in the presentation of new products by advertising, and even its reinforcing effect may have a serious social influence in the sense that the media have a fine disregard as to whether the tastes they reinforce are desirable or undesirable. But mass communications is not the brain-washing apparatus depicted and feared, and even its worst programs are not likely to have effects strong enough to lead to lives of crime and squalor.

As a matter of fact, studies seem to show that children who are heavy consumers of crime and violence on television are not significantly different from those who watch little or none of this sort of fare. Such children were found to be no more likely to engage in delinquent behavior, to be absent from school, or to achieve less. What was found, as might be expected, was that those who watch violent programs tend to be of a more aggressive nature than those who do not, but there is no evidence to show that the taste for violence was the result of the programs. In fact, some studies appear to show that the programs helped relieve tensions in such aggressive personalities.

How can we sum up the effects of mass communications, then? The following appear to be the findings:

1. Mass media must compete with many other forms of communication and many more powerful influences on individuals. Their effectiveness is thus rarely primary and varies widely among individuals and situations.

2. The content of mass communications is filtered through the background, experience, and preferences of the individual and serves generally only to reinforce existing opinions, attitudes, and tastes.

3. Mass media are nevertheless good and pervasive sources of information, and people often "hear it first," as the saying is, through radio, television, advertising, or the like.

4. In effecting change, mass media are only one of the many kinds of channels which play a role in the conversion process or process of acceptance, and it was found that each channel played a specific role and in a definite sequence. Thus, in a study of how doctors adopted a new drug, it was found that several channels played a part, that typically the doctor's first contact with the information on the drug was through commercial channels, while the additional information to which he attended had to come through professional sources. In another study of farmers' acceptance of a new fertilizer or a new kind of seed, it was shown that certain kinds of channels of information were associated with each of the four phases: the first in which the farmer became aware of the innovation, the second in which his interest was aroused, the third in which the decision was reached to accept, and the fourth in which he actually tried it out. It was found, indeed, that not only had different channels played the most important role in different phases but also that those farmers who had been exposed to the "wrong" channel at a given phase—for example, who had been made aware of the new practice by their neighbors rather than by the farm magazines—had

been more likely eventualy to reject the innovation than those who had been reached by the "right" channel at the "right" phase.

5. In persuasion, mass media play less of a role than face-to-face or interpersonal communication.

6. Finally, the effect of mass media is greater on disoriented persons or those cut off from their social group than on those who are part of an established order. During World War II, for example, it was found that propaganda appeals became effective on soldiers only after the military situation had led to the dissolution of primary groups to which the soldiers belonged.

Let us consider now our second set of questions on mass communications: Does not mass communications play a key role in binding the earth's peoples together; planing down the differences among men; standardizing tastes; increasing a similarity of viewpoint, values, and desires; and gradually converting the world into a single culture?

The answer, of course, must be in the affirmative. Mass communications, like the increased mobility afforded by modern transportation, is making the world one neighborhood. There is no question but that our mass media have carried the voices of the twentieth century on a world scale. Peoples and cultures, long slumbering out of the mainstream, are now speaking in the forum and hearing the dialogue of the major civilizations.

The effect of all this, it is said, is an increased standardization of the world, and it is felt that this is good in that it brings to all the fruits of knowledge, technology, new social and educational developments and improvements, and the arts, dreams, and aspirations of all. It is bad, others say, in that it promotes conformity and a loss of the fertile and necessary variety which stimulates human genius and achievement. The discussion is endless and perhaps academic, for whether good or bad, it is probably irreversible.

Second, instantaneous mass communications has brought a new immediacy and intensity to what is said. No news is old anymore. News can be transmitted to all as quickly as it happens. We live in the world now as in a town.

In the well-known words of formerly fashionable Marshall McLuhan: "As electrically contracted, the globe is no more than a village." This brings events anywhere in the world which could conceivably interest anyone to almost everyone as quickly and sometimes about as accurately as the village grapevine used to do. It means that the eye of the television camera and the ear of the radio are everywhere substituting not just for frontline reporting but for back-fence gossiping. It means that public figures can be and sometimes are more vivid to those in the mass audience, which of course means all of us, than even our own friends, and the fortunes of such public figures can be and often are as avidly followed as those of our own neighbors.

It means that no ideas or fashions can escape us anywhere in the world, nor can any change in those ideas or fashions. And it means that change comes fast. The latest dance, the latest craze, the latest smart personality, the latest important book, the latest smart phrase are with us all over the world within days and gone tomorrow. As Arthur Miller said: "Fashions which formerly took years to mature and fade away now appear, dominate and collapse in months or even weeks; the avant-garde is overtaken and institutionalized before it has had an hour of neglect to prove its purity." And it means that our cultural and material products will soon become as current and as old hat in Addis Ababa and in Zanzibar as they are in New York.

Again, the critics debate endlessly whether this is good or bad. Does it destroy small cultures of better quality or exalt them to world cultures? Does it produce a masscult which degrades all the high cultures of the world, or does it exalt the mass culture by incorporating into it the splendors, distinction, and individuality of high culture? Does it fill the world with trivial pseudoevents, or does it enrich the lives of ordinary people with the complexities and excitements of varied occurrences? Whatever it does, our interaction with our own culture has been tremendously speeded up, and our communication brings the world continuously and immediately within the range of our consciousness. And time itself has also speeded up the bringing to all fashions and events an increased ephemerality. Time's winged chariot is always with us now.

Third, our knowledge, information, and understanding of the world is tremendously richer in part because of mass communications, and this alone has certainly filled and enriched human life. "A single day among the learned," Seneca wrote, "lasts longer than the longest life of the ignorant." There are those who have pointed out that this enormous increase in the amount and availability of knowledge and the amount of this knowledge required to survive in this complex culture has placed heavy pressures and burdens on us and on our children, and the end is not yet in sight. But it is difficult to see how this kind of enrichment, whatever the pressures brought with it, can be anything but an unalloyed good. The life of a human being can be lived only through his culture, and the greater the knowledge and understanding this culture permits, the richer, the more profound, the more interesting his life. So, in this respect, we must credit mass communications with a profoundly beneficial effect and an even greater promise.

Finally, there are those who say mass communications has begun to change our world so profoundly that we are not yet fully aware of the real content of that change and have not yet caught up with it. We are always a step or so behind our new worlds, and it is the contention of a number of our sociologists and communication intellectuals that we have not faced up to our new environment or our new media.

THE VOICES OF THE FUTURE

So, we as business leaders and men of affairs must deal with the future, and we must deal with it now. We must listen to what the future is saying. What it seems to be saying is that we have been given a major task of great importance at this stage of the world's existence. We have been given the task of fulfilling the world's economic potential, not just for ourselves, not just for our own economies, but—if we and our economies are to survive—for all the peoples of the world, for humanity as a whole. This task requires more of us than we have heretofore been able to give. It requires a much larger view than business leaders in general have been able to develop. And it requires values that go even beyond the cherished values of a good profit and fair treatment to all who make up the economic complex.

It requires that the business leader look beyond his own field and his own interests and look at the major interests which concern the world—at poverty, illiteracy, injustice, fear, want, stupidity, and hatred. The business leader and man of affairs has been given great respect and power in our society because he is filling at this stage of our existence a crucial need—the need for food and economic security and the material things of the world. These are major goods which all the world can see and desire, but they are not the only major goods of life, and they cannot be effectively developed without regard to the other values men hold as paramount.

How then can the business leader and man of affairs listen to the future and understand what is expected of him, and how can he communicate that understanding? These are the questions which confront him, and they are just as important and in some respects even more important than those which confront him in his business operations. Today his voice must be heard, and he must take his place among other leaders in speaking out. And he must be talking about something that the world considers important, about the world's crucial problems, not only about his parochial interests. He must study the major trends of the world. He must be aware of what is going on in the major fields—in politics, in sociology, in science, in the arts, in education, in the world of the intellectual. These trends, these movements are not just sidelines to the main show; they are the main show. They are not just of peripheral interest to him; they are of primary concern, for he and his world may be dancing to those tunes, may be moving to the measures of that thinking. The future is being foretold now by that medley of voices, and the business leader must listen and listen carefully.

And finally, he must consider the content and the quality of what he has to offer to the world, and how best it can be communicated. Thus, we end as we began. The responsibility of the man of affairs has increased immeasurably today with the enormous potential extension of the sound of his voice and the reach of his thought through the modern means of transmission, the new mobility, the great increase in potential audience, the vast rise in general education, and the fact that the world is rapidly becoming one neighborhood. This new power and influence, therefore, place upon him a truly immense and untransferable burden, both social and moral—the necessity for a vast improvement in his style, his technique, his knowledgeability, and especially in the quality of what he says.

He cannot further afford to neglect or ignore the role that communicating plays in his influence on his society, for, if he is to make his full contributions, whether in business or in the great world, he must try to master that ultimate secret, the secret of reaching people, that crucial ability which Plato called "the art of ruling the minds of men."

ENVOI

IT HAS BEEN TEN YEARS SINCE THESE JOTTINGS were begun. The mystery of communicating, of reaching others remains as profound and inexplicable as it ever was. It is veiled in the mystery of human life and human consciousness and we are scarcely closer to solving it than when consciousness first dawned within us. All our studies of speech and language, of linguistics, of communications strategy, of the human brain, the human mind have brought us no closer to the powerful and disturbing secrets of memory and desire and the reaching into the lives of others.

These jottings, touching only bits and pieces, here and there, in the special area of the organization are like vague glimpses of the effects of some great force that can shape and influence the world and our own destinies. The theories of communicating, of reaching people that were popular when these jottings were first made have given way to other theories and so it will be, I believe, as long as we live and grow in this world.

On the practical side, since communicating is tied up with human personality, with how a person thinks of himself and sees himself, even with all the vast array of principles and techniques, each person must in the end learn how to reach others according to his own methods, and he must develop them and tailormake them out of his own life. No one can do this for him.

The executive like other leaders has risen in power, and, while he communicates pretty much the way everyone else does, because he affects people's careers and lives in a substantive way, he must take more responsibility and care in his communicating. He must give what he has to say more thought and weigh the consequences more carefully. Thus many leaders and not only in the business world say nothing in the right tone of voice and utter banalities or euphemisms and are damned as utter idiots and hypocritical blowhards for their pains. The truth is others can say what they want and even wittily but these privileged ones cannot.

Furthermore, in positions of power, the answers to complex questions, the solutions to conflicting situations, the right word, the revealing insight are hard to come by in the complexity of our economic strivings, and styles, values and conduct change as each generation enters the mainstream of life, while the leader, caught in the whirlwind must try to stand fast and represent what he was put there to represent. Usually, if what he represents must go the way of all flesh, he must go with it. As many men have died for words, the historian has noted, as for territory, but words are of no avail, when the great forces of the world require the changing of the guard.

Our efforts here to show how to reach others in organizations have only the validity that experience has given them, but experiences change and these techniques and values may change with them. We have built vast institutions to serve our needs and desires, and some of them, our contemporaries say, have overwhelmed us, have turned us into drudges, slaves and robots. No one, of course, can survive outside his culture, but it is salutary to remember after all that the corporate enterprise, the myriad voices, the cries and demands, the clamor of the world can disappear each night if we close our eyes, that no matter how powerful the message, how persuasive the commercial, the television set goes off at the turn of the switch, and that the single person with his life can be in the end the final arbiter of the world's values and demands and the ruler of his own mind. If we are to reach other minds we must be the ruler of our own.

Professor Annie Kriegel of the University of Paris has commented:

> Nothing is ever said once and for all. Nothing is ever learned beyond the need for relearning. Experience is not transmissible and the worst consequence of death is that it annihilates in one blow this form of primitive accumulation—acquired culture. . . .

Not quite.

Experience is to a degree transmissible, and it is acquired culture which has given us the power to reach other minds and thus in a sense to rule the world.

Index

263